About This Book

Why is this topic important?

Every decision we make has an emotional component. Every action we take, strategy we plan, budget we develop, and organizational restructuring we initiate has emotions at the core. Organizations in the past have encouraged their leaders and teams to stay logical and rational and not to let emotions get in the way of decisions that need to be made. Organizations today are recognizing that nothing makes more logical, rational sense than to acknowledge and develop, rather than ignore, emotional responses, as they are a key factor in all that leads to personal and organizational success. In fact, after IQ brings people to a job, emotional intelligence is a critical differentiator in success. Research also confirms that emotional intelligence skills can be learned. As these skills improve, so does the ability to influence, inspire, and motivate others and ourselves. We communicate better, more effectively manage stress and conflict, and ultimately achieve more when we invest in developing our emotional intelligence.

What can you achieve with this book?

Even with the explosion of interest in the business world regarding emotional intelligence, there are still very few resources available to guide professionals who are working with clients to help them develop their emotional intelligence skills. Fewer still are resources that highlight the leading-edge focus on team emotional and social intelligence presented by the Team Emotional and Social Intelligence Survey® (TESI®). The Emotional Intelligence Skills Assessment (EISA) also highlights key skills that impact both individual and team functioning. This book provides thirty-six exercises that target these skills. Written for coaches, trainers, facilitators, HR professionals, supervisors, and other leaders responsible for helping people achieve their best, the exercises are applicable to a wide variety of clients in both individual and team situations.

How is this book organized?

This book is organized into three parts. Part One provides guidance for practitioners to work with the book and an overview of the EISA and the TESI assessments. It also includes summaries of five additional widely used emotional intelligence, personality, and leadership assessments and a matrix linking every exercise in this book to the competencies measured by all seven of these instruments. Part Two provides experiential exercises to develop effective emotional intelligence skills built around the five individual emotional intelligence factors measured by the EISA. Part Three presents experiential exercises to develop effective team emotional and social skills built around the seven team competencies measured by the TESI.

About Pfeiffer

Pfeiffer serves the professional development and hands-on resource needs of training and human resource practitioners and gives them products to do their jobs better. We deliver proven ideas and solutions from experts in HR development and HR management, and we offer effective and customizable tools to improve workplace performance. From novice to seasoned professional, Pfeiffer is the source you can trust to make yourself and your organization more successful.

Essential Knowledge Pfeiffer produces insightful, practical, and comprehensive materials on topics that matter the most to training and HR professionals. Our Essential Knowledge resources translate the expertise of seasoned professionals into practical, how-to guidance on critical workplace issues and problems. These resources are supported by case studies, worksheets, and job aids and are frequently supplemented with CD-ROMs, websites, and other means of making the content easier to read, understand, and use.

Essential Tools Pfeiffer's Essential Tools resources save time and expense by offering proven, ready-to-use materials—including exercises, activities, games, instruments, and assessments—for use during a training or team-learning event. These resources are frequently offered in looseleaf or CD-ROM format to facilitate copying and customization of the material.

Pfeiffer also recognizes the remarkable power of new technologies in expanding the reach and effectiveness of training. While e-hype has often created whizbang solutions in search of a problem, we are dedicated to bringing convenience and enhancements to proven training solutions. All our e-tools comply with rigorous functionality standards. The most appropriate technology wrapped around essential content yields the perfect solution for today's on-the-go trainers and human resource professionals.

Essential resources for training and HR professionals

www.pfeiffer.com

Developing Emotional and Social Intelligence

Exercises for Leaders, Individuals, and Teams

MARCIA HUGHES

AMY MILLER

Building your capacity to work with leaders and teams using the EISA, the TESI® and many other strategies.

Pfeiffer
A Wiley Imprint
www.pfeiffer.com

Published by Pfeiffer

An Imprint of Wiley

989 Market Street, San Francisco, CA 94103-1741

www.pfeiffer.com

For additional copies/bulk purchases of this book in the U.S. please contact 800-274-4434.

Pfeiffer books and products are available through most bookstores. To contact Pfeiffer directly call our Customer Care Department within the U.S. at 800-274-4434, outside the U.S. at 317-572-3985, fax 317-572-4002, or visit www.pfeiffer.com.

Pfeiffer also publishes its books in a variety of electronic formats. Some content that appears in print may not be available in electronic books.

Library of Congress Cataloging-in-Publication Data

Hughes, Marcia M.

    Developing emotional and social intelligence : exercises for leaders, individuals, and teams / Marcia Hughes, Amy Miller.

      p. cm.

  Summary: "Emotional Intelligence has been proven to be key to leadership success. In this book, EI expert Marcia Hughes provides a broad array of activities for developing EI in both the coaching and team environment. All of these activities have stood the test of time and will help trainers at all levels engage the learner in active, experiential learning. Additionally, there are introductions to each activity that provide tips and techniques that will ensure success every time. The activities are organized with separate sections for individual coaching and team development"—Provided by publisher.

    ISBN 978-0-470-54702-1 (pbk.)

    1. Emotional intelligence. 2. Social intelligence. 3. Leadership. 4. Executive coaching. I. Miller, Amy, II. Title.

    BF576.H84 2010

    658.3'124—dc22

                                                2010021349

Acquiring Editor: Holly J. Allen

Director of Development: Kathleen Dolan Davies

Production Editor: Dawn Kilgore

Editor: Rebecca Taff

Editorial Assistant: Lindsay Morton

Manufacturing Supervisor: Becky Morgan

Printed in the United States of America

Printing   10 9 8 7 6 5 4 3 2 1

This book is dedicated to all of the practitioners in the world, no matter what their professional title or role, who seek to help people improve the quality of human relationships. We believe that developing the ability to consciously engage one's own emotional energy harmoniously with others' will be the gift that allows civilization to achieve sustainability in its many forms that touch us at the body, mind, heart, and soul levels.

Contents

On the Web

The following materials are available for download from www.pfeiffer.com/go/marciahughes
password: training

Part Two

Emotional Congruence Handout
Emotions Bingo Handout
Emotions Bingo Handout (Facilitator Copy)
Acknowledging Ambivalence Handout

Success in Managing Emotions Handout
From Emotional Intensity to Curiosity Handout
The Essential Conversation Handout

Emotions Inform Decisions Handout
Who's in Control—You or Your Impulses? Developing Self-Mastery Handout
Decision Making, Emotions, and Thinking Styles Handout

Emotional Well-Being Handout
Collaborating Handout

Be a Magnet Handout
Engaged Listening Handout
Achieve Your G.O.A.L. with Effective Feedback Handout

Part Three

Acknowledgments

The authors wish to acknowledge and thank all of the following people:

The many coaches, coachees, teams, and organizations with whom we have had the great honor to work. You teach us daily.

Steven Stein, James Buchanan, Diana Durek, and all our brilliant colleagues at Multi-Health Systems who promote emotional intelligence daily. Reuven Bar-On, Peter Salovey, John D. Mayer, David R. Caruso, Daniel Goleman, Cary Cherniss, Richard E. Boyatzis, and Annie McKee for your pioneering emotional intelligence work.

Claudia Busch Lee of Catalyst Consulting Inc., for helping to develop three and edit several of the exercises and for her zest in bringing the best to all her training and coaching.

Holly J. Allen, senior acquisitions editor; Tolu Babalola, marketing manager; Susan Rachmeler, senior development editor; Dawn Kilgore, production editor; Lindsay Morton, editorial assistant; Marisa Kelley, assistant editor; and Rebecca Taff, manuscript editor, for all the professional effort and detail it takes to make a very good book! Michael Snell, our agent, for creating an excellent interface with our publisher, orchestrating a win-win process, and making it fun as we continue down the publishing path. We also thank Jennifer Hunt for her consistently cheerful attitude, commitment to quality, and diligent support in keeping the administrative details together.

Marcia wishes to thank her extraordinary husband and business partner, James Terrell, and her daughter, Julia, who continues to support her work in contributing to the effective evolution of building emotional intelligence in the world. Amy thanks her treasured family—Jim and Alyce, Laura and Cory, Keith, Lindsey, and Travis, Peter and Eli—for being the best teachers, coaches, mentors, and consultants anyone could dream of having.

Introduction

The gifts offered by emotional and social intelligence (ESI) make a long-lasting difference in one's life. It is no exaggeration to say that the skills displayed through the artful use of ESI are exactly what the world needs now. We are faced with global challenges related to life on all dimensions: personal, business, health, community, and the environment. There can be no doubt that we need all the resources possible. ESI offers the ability to comprehend how we feel so we can better understand and manage our emotions, communications, and motivations. It offers the ability to develop effective and sustainable relationships. Good relationships are the beginning point for collaboration, and surely we must work together to address the challenges we face at the individual, local, and global levels.

Emotions are energizers. They lead us to move toward what we want, away from that which we do not want, and against that which we fear or oppose. They are the source of our deciding what we do or do not want. People respond to emotions on a continuous basis. They don't have any choice; it's a fundamental part of human hardwiring. However, people do have choice about how they respond. Emotional skills can be deliberately learned and cultivated. Leaders, teams, trainers, coaches, and facilitators, all of whom are engaged in the effort to support people in making the most effective choices for themselves and others, must work with developing and focusing emotional and social intelligence skills in order to be effective. Emotions inform decisions; that cannot be avoided. But how emotions inform decisions can be intentionally chosen. Those choices are instrumental in meeting today's challenges.

Businesses, governments, non-profits, truly all types of organizations, are incorporating ESI in leadership development, coaching, team building and many other formats. The data demonstrating the direct tie to improving the bottom line and overall effectiveness can be found in many sources, such as the business case information available at www.eiconsortium.org. Neurologists have demonstrated that we can't make decisions without accessing emotional data. In fact the emotional response kicks in just before our more deliberative thinking processes do. That's why we were taught to count to ten in elementary school before we said something we might regret. So emotions will affect our decisions, but whether that emotional information will be used effectively is up for grabs. If someone is unaware of his or her feelings or doesn't know how to manage them, or if someone is unaware of how others feel and how to respond effectively to the emotions of others, he or she is in trouble. It is not just a matter of not performing at their best, but most likely that negative consequences are occurring. And these consequences are not necessary. ESI skills development is what is needed. This book is designed to be a powerful tool to assist in that change. Leaders and individuals need to use and expand their ESI, and teams are required to learn to work together more effectively than ever.

This book provides thirty-six exercises designed to support practitioners, leaders, and teams in building ESI skills to meet any challenges they may face. Anyone can increase his or her emotional and social intelligence if the desire and resources exist. This creates an exciting and motivating can-do set of possibilities. However, success requires personal or team awareness, a personal commitment to grow, a willingness to practice and, frequently, help from a coach or facilitator skilled in supporting that development. We have designed a wide range of exercises so there are choices to draw on by those of different skill levels, from beginning to advanced.

Resources are available to support your use of these exercises in trainings. Agendas and other training support are available in two facilitator's guides published by Pfeiffer. For the *Team Emotional and Social Intelligence*

Survey® (TESI®) check out Hughes and Terrell (2009). To find agendas and other support material for training with the *Emotional Intelligence Skills Assessment*, check out Stein, Mann, Papadogiannis, and Gordon (2009).

If you are new to working with ESI, we anticipate you will be excited at the welcome results you will find. As the more advanced ESI users will tell you, participating in individual and team development is so gratifying that we strongly suspect you will want to work with it more and more. You can consult many resources to further your understanding in this field. One that addresses developmental ideas for working with many of the assessments discussed in this book is the *Handbook for Developing Emotional and Social Intelligence* (Hughes, Thompson, & Terrell, 2009). *Emotional Intelligence in Action* (Hughes, Patterson, & Terrell, 2005) also includes forty-six exercises organized around the EQ-i® and with a cross-reference for other assessments. If you want to bring in more exercises to choose from, these two resources work together well.

When working with these exercises, take time to understand your audience, your goals, and the skills you need. By assembling the right client data and combining it with a thoughtful approach, you will have many opportunities to support long-term, sustainable growth. The results are rewarding and renewing. We wish you and the many people you work with great success. The world will be a better place for your efforts.

Developing Emotional and Social Intelligence with Individuals and Teams

CHAPTER 1

Getting the Most from This Resource

PURPOSE

There is a growing appreciation for the power of emotional intelligence and the role it plays in life success, both at home and at work. One of the most encouraging aspects about emotional intelligence is that it can be learned and improved. Instead of being a static trait, emotional intelligence is comprised of competencies and skills that can be enhanced over time. Almost everyone can become better at recognizing and managing their emotions, at applying their increased awareness and improved behaviors more effectively to a greater range of situations, and at enhancing their interactions with others in individual and team situations. They will achieve greater success as a result. The purpose of this book is to help leaders, teams, organizations, and the skilled professionals who work with them to take advantage of the opportunities in improving leader and team emotional intelligence.

AUDIENCE

This book is designed for anyone who wants to help others improve their emotional intelligence: coaches, trainers, facilitators, HR professionals, supervisors, and other leaders responsible for helping people achieve their best will find exercises to guide their work. Most exercises are effective for individual clients as well as teams and groups. Whether written with an individual or a team focus, many of the exercises can be easily modified so that they meet the developmental needs of team leaders, of individuals in a coaching session or group training, of individual team members desiring to build skills to take back to the team, and of intact teams.

The exercises can serve as valuable contributions for those offering open trainings for individuals or teams interested in developing competencies in emotional and social intelligence, improving relationships, expanding their career development opportunities, and building life skills. Additionally, the exercises can be useful in clinical applications with clients where the focus includes developing emotional intelligence to achieve therapeutic goals.

ASSESSMENTS

Emotional intelligence does not have to be formally assessed before one can set goals for improvement. Professionals wanting to help their clients learn how to better manage their emotions, improve their decision making, more effectively influence others, or enhance team performance can turn immediately to any page in this book and find exercises that will help them do so.

For those practitioners who are considering the use of assessments to measure their individual clients' or teams' emotional and social functioning, several resources in this book will be of assistance. The exercises are developed specifically to enhance the emotional intelligence factors that are measured by two powerful assessments: the *Emotional Intelligence Skills Assessment* (EISA), which measures individual emotional intelligence according to five skill areas, and the Team Emotional and Social Intelligence (TESI) assessment, which measures team emotional intelligence according to seven skill areas. These assessments identify a combined twelve key areas of functioning, and this book presents exercises that correlate to those twelve key competencies. More is written about these competencies and the two assessments throughout this book, including in the next chapter on assessments you might use. Moreover, at the beginning of each skill covered in Parts Two and Three is an overview of that particular skill. You will also learn more from descriptions in the individual exercises.

Many who use assessments with their clients understand the power of administering multiple assessments. No one instrument can measure everything about a person. Incorporating a variety of perspectives helps create a more complete picture. Assessment results that combine to highlight clear themes and patterns in clients' functioning provide greater understanding for clients. This deeper cognitive awareness also helps generate the emotions essential to successful personal development—hope, motivation, encouragement, to name just a few—that lead to greater achievement.

The exercises in this book, therefore, also link to competencies measured by other assessments. Readers who use or are considering the use of assessments in addition to the EISA or TESI will find that the exercises provide opportunities for developing competencies measured by a number of other instruments, particularly the Emotional Quotient Inventory® (EQ-i®) and its 360-degree version, the EQ-360®; the *Leadership Practices Inventory* (LPI); the Myers-Briggs Type Indicator® (MBTI®); Emergenetics®; and the Fundamental Interpersonal Relations Orientation-Behavior® (FIRO-B®). These assessments are described in Chapter 2 and are followed by a cross-referenced matrix that assists in identifying which exercises link to which competencies in the assessments. For example, learning to be more expressive is a frequent client goal. The skill of expressiveness is a facet within the extraversion dimension of the MBTI, a behavioral component in Emergenetics, and linked to other skills in the EISA, TESI, EQ-i, LPI, and FIRO-B. You will find ways to build expressiveness in Exercises 8.1, 9.1, 9.2, and 10.1 (and others) in this book and that can be done in conjunction with the assessment of your choice.

HOW THIS BOOK IS ORGANIZED

This book is organized into three parts. Part One, Developing Emotional and Social Intelligence with Individuals and Teams, is described above. It contains information about the EISA and the TESI, an overview of the five other widely used assessments named above, and the matrix linking every exercise in this book to the competencies measured by all seven of these assessments.

Part Two, Exercises to Use in Developing Emotionally Intelligent Leaders and Individuals, is built upon the organization of the EISA. Five sections each begin with an in-depth description of one of the five EISA factors—Perceiving, Managing, Decision Making, Achieving, and Influencing—and are followed by experiential exercises designed to develop those skills.

Part Three, Exercises to Build Emotionally Intelligent Teams, is based on the seven emotional and social competencies of the TESI. Seven sections each begin with an in-depth description of one of the seven TESI skills—Team Identity, Motivation, Emotional Awareness, Communication, Stress Tolerance, Conflict Resolution, and Positive Mood. These sections are then followed by experiential exercises designed to develop the team's skills in these areas.

The Appendix provides an extensive vocabulary of feeling words. Be sure to consult this list frequently. Sample emotion words are offered in many of the exercises. You can substitute different words that work better for your context by referring to the Appendix.

Also included is a Resources list, which identifies some of the many places you may find additional useful information.

GUIDELINES FOR FACILITATORS

Preparation and Selection

Emotional intelligence competencies frequently build upon and interact with each other; therefore many of the exercises in this book will provide opportunities for clients to develop a number of related emotional intelligence skills. However, each exercise is designed to target one particular skill. It is valuable for practitioners to understand emotional intelligence before identifying competencies, choosing exercises, and leading individual and team clients in exercises that will help them enhance these skills. Here are some suggested steps for facilitators:

- Read applicable materials to educate yourself on the area you will be addressing. You'll find some ideas in the Resources list and the References at the back of the book.
- Review the appropriate sections in Part Two and Part Three to better understand the emotional intelligence skill on which you might be asking your clients to focus.
- Review results from other administered assessments, if any, to help identify additional competencies that might correlate with the EISA and TESI competencies in Parts Two and Three.
- Refer to the cross-referenced matrix in Chapter 2 to identify the exercise(s) you might want to use.
- Find the potential exercises you identified from the cross-referenced matrix. Review the purpose, thumbnail, outcome, audience, estimated time, and facilitator competency information to help you identify the best exercise(s) for your situation. The paragraphs below provide more details about each section in the exercises so that you will know where to look quickly to find the information to determine whether the exercise is appropriate for your needs.
- Review the exercise more thoroughly to confirm that it is appropriate for you and your clients.
- Ensure the room size and table arrangements are conducive to the type of exercise you will be leading.
- Gather needed materials and make sufficient copies of any reproducible participant handouts that are included in the exercise. Full-size versions of the handouts are available at www.pfeiffer.com/go/marciahughes (password: training)

Exercise Format

The exercises in Part Two and Part Three follow the same format. The first sections of each exercise—Purpose, Thumbnail, and Outcome—explain the following:

- Purpose answers WHY you would select the exercise to use with your clients;

- Thumbnail tells you HOW participants will engage with the instructional material to generate the learning experience and how much time should be allowed for the exercise; and
- Outcome explains WHAT desired results can be achieved.

The exercises and the supporting website (www.pfeiffer.com/go/marciahughes) contain reproducible handouts that you may copy for your participants.

The Audience section indicates whether the exercise is written with an individual or team focus or can be adapted to work with both. The clients may be intact teams, team leaders, individual team members desiring to build skills to take back to the team, individuals working with a coach or team leader, or a group of individuals such as in leadership development training. Most of the exercises can be used for a variety of client groups and situations.

The Facilitator Competencies section indicates what level of skill the practitioner needs in order to successfully conduct the exercise. This level will generally also reflect the level of sophistication of the learning experience for the participants. If participants' skills tend to be less developed in an area, starting with an easier exercise will likely provide better results.

There are five levels of facilitator skills identified:

 Easy

 Easy to Moderate

 Moderate

 Moderate to Advanced

 Advanced

The Materials section in each exercise lists all materials needed to conduct the exercise, including participant handouts. These handouts are shown at the end of the exercise; full-size versions are also available on the website for the book.

The Time Matrix provides an outline of the key actions within each exercise and a time estimate for how long each exercise will take to complete. These estimates are just a guideline. Times may vary depending on the size and nature of the team. When working with an individual, some exercises may take even longer, as the more intimate setting may encourage a deeper discussion.

The Instructions section provides step-by-step details for the successful facilitation of the exercise. This section is written with the assumption that the practitioner has general skills in leading exercises but not specific knowledge about the actual exercise. Where appropriate, some exercises include suggestions for "stretch goals" for situations with clients who are ready for more growth opportunities.

Feedback and Reflection

Providing direct feedback, sometimes referred to as debriefing, is one of the most important phases of the exercises. It gives participants the opportunity to reflect on and synthesize their experiences and to share what they have learned. It challenges them to develop additional emotional intelligence skills, as they will need to focus on their emotional response to what has happened in order to participate in the discussion. Taking time to reflect is one of the best opportunities for introverts to be heard and is essential for anyone who truly wants to integrate the learning opportunities.

Every exercise has been designed to generate an emotional experience for all participants. The discussions that you will be facilitating during and after the exercises are therefore crucial because that is where much learning, understanding, practicing, and integration of new skills will take place. Your thoughtful inquiry regarding participants' emotional response to the exercise(s) will challenge them to develop additional social and emotional intelligence skills such as team motivation, communication, conflict resolution, and stress tolerance as they work to articulate their experience with the exercise(s). We also suggest you check other resources to build your understanding of the topics, such as *A Coach's Guide to Emotional Intelligence* (Terrell & Hughes, 2008). Your job as the facilitator is to ask thought-provoking questions and to create the safest environment possible for these discussions to happen, including periods of silence that will encourage even the quietest participants to share.

CHAPTER 2

Supporting Your ESI Work
Using Assessments

T he exercises in this book are presented to support your work in developing emotional intelligence in leaders and teams. The skills and competencies required can be addressed with or without the use of an assessment. Assessments can increase awareness and motivation for change, so we find that gaining the data and clarifications from credible assessments is a great strategy for success. Should you wish to use an assessment, we have described several that work well with the exercises in this book. We have organized the exercises around skills for individuals and teams as measured by two well-respected emotional intelligence instruments, the Emotional Intelligence Skills Assessment (EISA) and the Team Emotional and Social Intelligence (TESI) assessment. These are described briefly below and in greater detail in the chapters that follow.

In addition to the EISA and the TESI, a wide variety of assessments have been developed over the years to measure personality, leadership styles, change management, emotional intelligence, and interpersonal relationship behaviors that assist individuals and teams in enhancing their functioning.

The exercises in this book can be used to support the development efforts of competencies that are measured by other individual and team assessments. This chapter describes several of these respected assessments and includes a cross-referenced matrix that suggests the exercises that best support various competencies measured by these additional instruments. The assessments included are the Emotional Quotient Inventory® (EQ-i®) and its 360-degree version, the EQ-360®; the *Leadership Practices Inventory* (LPI); the Myers-Briggs Type Indicator® (MBTI®); Emergenetics®; and the Fundamental Interpersonal Relations Orientation-Behavior® (FIRO-B®).

The descriptions below provide brief summaries of each model. For more complete information, please review the materials provided by the authors and their publishers.

EMOTIONAL INTELLIGENCE SKILLS ASSESSMENT (EISA)

The *Emotional Intelligence Skills Assessment* (EISA), developed by Steven Stein, Derek Mann, and Peter Papadogiannis (2009), identifies and measures five core factors of emotional intelligence in adults: Perceiving, Managing, Decision Making, Achieving, and Influencing. While all five factors are important, the first two—Perceiving and Managing—are considered foundational to emotional intelligence, as without the ability to accurately perceive and manage one's own emotions, it is more difficult to respond appropriately to situations requiring effective Decision Making, Achieving, and Influencing.

The EISA asks each individual to respond to fifty emotional and behavioral statements; both self and 360 versions of the assessment are available. Individuals receive detailed information about each of the five factors and an indication of their areas of emotional strength and opportunities for growth. Respondents are also encouraged to create a plan that will help them further develop those emotional and social skills needed for improved success.

More information about each of the five factors, along with exercises for developing Perceiving, Managing, Decision Making, Achieving, and Influencing skills, is provided in Part Two of this book. In addition, the *EISA Facilitator's Guide* is a valuable resource for more information on this assessment.

TEAM EMOTIONAL AND SOCIAL INTELLIGENCE (TESI)

The Team Emotional and Social Intelligence (TESI) assessment, developed in 2006 by Marcia Hughes and James Terrell, identifies and measures seven competencies most critical for effective team functioning: Team Identity, Motivation, Emotional Awareness, Communication, Stress Tolerance, Conflict Resolution, and Positive Mood. It also specifies the four results that teams will enjoy as they build these competencies—Empathy, Trust, Loyalty, and Better Decisions—which lead to the two benefits of long-term success, Sustainable Productivity and Emotional and Social Well-Being for the team (Hughes & Terrell, 2007, 2009).

Each of the seven skills for team success influences the other; skills in one area flow into and build a positive influence in each of the others. In addition, synergistic results are achieved when a team strengthens competencies in most or all of these core areas. Their success becomes greater than the simple combination of each independent skill, building what Hughes and Terrell term Collaborative Intelligence™ (Hughes & Terrell, 2009).

There are two assessment formats available. The TESI Short is an abbreviated, twenty-one-item version of this assessment and is published by Pfeiffer. The short version works well when teams want to take a quick look at their functioning. It's available in a self-scoring format that creates the flexibility of not having to administer it in advance of a team engagement or workshop. A longer version of the TESI with demographic and other breakouts is available from Collaborative Growth®. Each member is asked to rate the team's skills—from his or her individual perspective—in the seven team behaviors of success. An individual report is created, as well as the full team report and many optional demographic reports. This serves to create a team 360-degree assessment of all team members' views on team functioning. From this report, participants better understand the team's functioning and take steps to build upon their strengths and develop areas needing enhancement.

Part Three of this book provides more detailed information about the TESI's seven core competencies and exercises for developing skills in each of them.

ADDITIONAL ASSESSMENTS

In addition to correlating to the EISA and TESI competencies, the exercises in this book apply to concepts and competencies in many other individual and organizational assessments. Virtually any instrument that assesses interpersonal skills, emotional intelligence, team dynamics, personality style, conflict management, or change style could well have skill areas that can be enhanced by exercises in this book.

Five widely administered assessments that reflect aspects of emotional effectiveness include the EQ-i/EQ-360, LPI, MBTI, Emergenetics, and FIRO-B. Here is a brief description of each of these assessments, followed by a summary matrix to suggest which exercises in this book can be incorporated when using these other instruments with clients to enhance emotional and social effectiveness to improve individual and team functioning.

Emotional Quotient Inventory (EQ-i) and EQ-360

The Emotional Quotient Inventory (EQ-i) and the corresponding EQ-360 (multi-rater instrument) are robust, statistically validated, and reliable tools for measuring emotional intelligence (Bar-On, 2004). In 1980, Dr. Reuven Bar-On began looking for factors related to success in life and tried to understand why some people with a moderate IQ do well in life while others with a high IQ fail. He discovered that emotional and social functioning determined the difference and developed an instrument to measure emotional and social effectiveness and to predict emotionally intelligent behavior in the future.

In worldwide use for many years, the EQ-i provides an overall Emotional Quotient score as well as scores on five composite areas and fifteen subscale skills. These composite scales, with their corresponding subscales, include:

- Intrapersonal
  - Self-Regard
  - Emotional Self-Awareness
  - Independence
  - Assertiveness
  - Self-Actualization

- Interpersonal
  - Empathy
  - Social Responsibility
  - Interpersonal Relationships
- Stress Management
  - Stress Tolerance
  - Impulse Control
- Adaptability
  - Reality Testing
  - Flexibility
  - Problem Solving
- General Mood
  - Optimism
  - Happiness
  (Bar-On, 2004, pp. 112–117)

Leadership Practices Inventory (LPI)

The Leadership Practices Inventory (LPI) is a 360-degree assessment developed as a result of extensive research by James Kouzes and Barry Posner, best-selling authors of *The Leadership Challenge* (Kouzes & Posner, 2007). Their research identified five practices that support effective leadership, and the LPI provides a tool that helps leaders assess the extent to which they apply these practices.

Two of the many important contributions made by Kouzes' and Posner's research are their conclusions (1) that leadership can be learned and (2) that effective leadership practices are universal. Individuals worldwide can and do learn to become better leaders by adjusting their behavior to follow The Five Practices of Exemplary Leadership®. Many of these practices include components that are considered crucial skills and behaviors for effective social and emotional functioning as well.

The Five Practices of Exemplary Leadership and some of the corresponding behaviors, detailed in *The Leadership Challenge* (Kouzes & Posner, 2007, pp. vii–ix), include:

1. Model the Way
   - Clarify Values—Find Your Voice, Affirm Shared Values

- Set the Example—Personify the Shared Values, Teach Others to Model the Values
2. Inspire a Shared Vision
   - Envision the Future—Imagine the Possibilities, Find a Common Purpose
   - Enlist Others—Appeal to Common Ideals, Animate the Vision
3. Challenge the Process
   - Search for Opportunities—Seize the Initiative, Exercise Outsight
   - Experiment and Take Risks—Generate Small Wins, Learn from Experience
4. Enable Others to Act
   - Foster Collaboration—Create a Climate of Trust, Facilitate Relationships
   - Strengthen Others—Enhance Self-Determination, Develop Competence and Confidence
5. Encourage the Heart
   - Recognize Contributions—Expect the Best, Personalize Recognition
   - Celebrate the Values and Victories—Create a Spirit of Community, Be Personally Involved

Myers-Briggs Type Indicator (MBTI)

The Myers-Briggs Type Indicator (MBTI) is a widely used self-report assessment that was developed to help measure and appreciate normal personality differences among healthy people. Over sixty years of research and development by Katherine Cook Briggs, her daughter Isabel Briggs Myers, and those who later built on their work have provided a rich foundation for understanding the mental and behavioral preferences people express in their everyday lives.

Based on Carl Jung's theory of psychological type, and as described in *Introduction to Type*, by Isabel Briggs Myers (1998), the MBTI measures individual preferences along four dimensions: where people focus their attention and gain energy (Extraversion or Introversion); how they take in information (Sensing or Intuition); how they make decisions (Thinking or Feeling); and how they orient themselves to the outer world (Judging or Perceiving) (Myers, 1998, pp. 8–10). Later expansion on Myers' research into more specific clusters of behavior led to the MBTI Form Q, with Step II scoring, which identifies an additional set of measurable behaviors (facets) within each of the main preferences scales.

The preferences, along each of the four dimensions, create a possibility of sixteen unique and equally valued personality types. Each type is dynamic and represents more than just the sum of the individual dimensions of which it is comprised. This is true of the facets as well; the specific behaviors help describe general, common responses, but how each individual blends preferences into overall behaviors is what adds depth and richness to the theory.

Combined, these behaviors and the psychological types that they reflect provide a strong foundation for understanding the healthy differences among people. This understanding is crucial for developing emotional and social skills, as emotional effectiveness requires an ability to respond to each person in a way that best meets that individual's unique needs. The MBTI offers a valuable opportunity to first understand one's own, and others', unique needs before one develops skills to respond to them.

The four dimensions and their corresponding twenty behavioral facets include:

- Extraversion/Introversion
  - Initiating/Receiving
  - Expressive/Contained
  - Gregarious/Intimate
  - Active/Reflective
  - Enthusiastic/Quiet
- Sensing/Intuition
  - Concrete/Abstract
  - Realistic/Imaginative
  - Practical /Conceptual
  - Experiential/Theoretical
  - Traditional/Original
- Thinking/Feeling
  - Logical/Empathetic
  - Reasonable/Compassionate
  - Questioning/Accommodating

- Critical/Accepting
- Tough/Tender
- Judging/Perceiving
  - Systematic/Casual
  - Planful/Open-Ended
  - Early Starting/Pressure-Prompted
  - Scheduled/Spontaneous
  - Methodical/Emergent

(Myers, 1998, p. 41)

Emergenetics

Emergenetics, developed by Geil Browning and Wendell Williams, reflects their theory that "Who you are today is a result of certain characteristics that have *emerged* from your life experiences, plus the *genetics* with which you were born . . . this interplay between nature and nurture [is] *Emergenetics*" (Browning, 2006, p. 6).

Emergenetics' focus is on behavioral and thinking preferences, which provides valuable insights into how and why people think and respond in the ways they do. These insights are the foundation for building effective emotional and social skills. Emergenetics helps individuals develop awareness of themselves and others, leading to greater abilities to manage interpersonal interactions.

The Emergenetics assessment measures individual thinking and behavioral styles, based on scientific research into traits—those personality characteristics with which we are born—and how those traits can be modified as we respond to environmental events throughout our lives. The Emergenetics report includes information about four thinking attributes—Analytical, Conceptual, Structural, and Social—as well as three behavioral attributes—Expressiveness, Assertiveness, and Flexibility. Combined, these seven thinking and behavioral attributes comprise an individual's profile. These styles are reported as preferences, not abilities, with each style and individual profile having corresponding strengths and challenges. The thinking preference characteristics include:

- *Analytical*: clear thinker, logical problem solver, enjoys math, rational, learns by mental analysis

- *Structural*: practical thinker, likes guidelines, cautious of new ideas, predictable, learns by doing
- *Conceptual*: imaginative, intuitive about ideas, visionary, enjoys the unusual, learns by experimenting
- *Social*: intuitive about people, socially aware, sympathetic, empathic, learns from others

The behavioral attributes (listed on a spectrum from lower to higher frequency of behavior) include:

- *Expressiveness*: quiet, alone, reserved, spontaneous, gregarious
- *Assertiveness*: peacekeeper, amiable, easy-going, competitive, driving, telling
- *Flexibility*: defined situations, strong opinions, different points of view, others before self
  (Browning, 2006, pp. 53, 86–87)

Fundamental Interpersonal Relations Orientation–Behavior (FIRO-B)

The Fundamental Interpersonal Relations Orientation–Behavior (FIRO-B) instrument is another valuable tool in understanding the variety of ways individuals respond, and want to be responded to, in their interactions with others.

Developed by Dr. Will Schutz over fifty years ago, this fifty-four-item, self-report assessment measures three interpersonal needs—Inclusion, Control, and Affection—and the degree to which individuals express, and want others to express, behaviors that meet those needs. Combined, the scores representing these various needs and behaviors help illuminate the basis on which people develop their perceptions of each other.

Dr. Schutz believed these needs for Inclusion, Control, and Affection to be as motivating as humans' biological survival needs of food, clothing, and shelter (Waterman & Rogers, 2004). Understanding the role and nature of these interpersonal needs is therefore crucial to enhancing emotional and social effectiveness. With this understanding, one is far more likely to experience positive and successful interactions with others. Without it, conflicts often develop between individuals who are not perceiving or responding to each other's needs for Inclusion, Control, and Affection.

There are no right or wrong FIRO-B scores. The value in the instrument is that one gains an understanding of the wide variety of interpersonal behaviors and needs that exist among people, which enhances one's awareness and ability to more effectively interact with others in ways in which they are most comfortable.

Finally, FIRO-B theory suggests that while individuals may have natural tendencies for how they respond to situations, they also can change their

Connecting the Exercises with the Assessments

Exercise	Page	EISA	TESI	EQi	
				Composite	Subscale
3.1 Emotional Congruence	39	Perceiving	Team Emotional Awareness Team Communication	Intrapersonal Interpersonal Adaptability	Emotional Self-Awareness Empathy Interpersonal Relationships Reality Testing
3.2 Emotions Bingo	43	Perceiving	Team Emotional Awareness Team Communication	All	Emotional Self-Awareness Empathy Interpersonal Relationships Impulse Control Reality Testing Flexibility Optimism Happiness
3.3 Acknowledging Ambivalence	48	Perceiving	Team Motivation Team Emotional Awareness Team Communication Team Conflict Resolution	Intrapersonal Interpersonal Adaptability	Emotional Self-Awareness Empathy Interpersonal Relationships Impulse Control Reality Testing Flexibility Optimism

behaviors based on life experiences and individual choice. Therefore, FIRO-B scores may change as new skills are developed or as life situations change (Waterman & Rogers, 2004).

CONNECTING THESE ASSESSMENTS WITH THE EXERCISES

The matrix on the following pages links every exercise in this book to the competencies measured by all seven of the assessments described above.

LPI	MBTI		Emergenetics		FIRO-B
Practice	Dimension	Facet	Thinking	Behavioral	Need
All	Extraversion Introversion Feeling	Expressive Reflective Empathetic	Social Analytical	Expressiveness Assertiveness	Inclusion Affection
Enable Others to Act	Extraversion Introversion Sensing Intuition Feeling Perceiving	Expressive Reflective Experiential Conceptual Empathetic Compassionate Accepting Spontaneous	Social Analytical Conceptual	Expressiveness Flexibility	All
All	Introversion Feeling	Reflective Empathetic Accepting	Social Analytical	Expressiveness Flexibility	All

(Continued)

Connecting the Exercises with the Assessments (*continued*)

		EISA	TESI	EQi	
Exercise	Page			Composite	Subscale
4.1 Success in Managing Emotions	59	Managing	All	All	Emotional Self-Awareness Empathy Interpersonal Relationships Impulse Control Reality Testing Flexibility Optimism Happiness
4.2 From Emotional Intensity to Curiosity	64	Managing	Team Emotional Awareness Team Stress Tolerance Team Conflict Resolution	Intrapersonal Stress Management Adaptability General Mood	Emotional Self-Awareness Impulse Control Reality Testing Happiness
4.3 The Essential Conversation	70	Managing	Team Emotional Awareness Team Communication Team Conflict Resolution	All	Emotional Self-Awareness Assertiveness Social Responsibility Interpersonal Relationships Impulse Control Reality Testing Problem Solving Optimism
5.1 Emotions Inform Decisions	79	Decision Making	Team Emotional Awareness	Intrapersonal Adaptability General Mood	Emotional Self-Awareness Reality Testing Problem Solving Optimism
5.2 Who's in Control – You or Your Impulses? Developing Self-Mastery	84	Decision Making	Team Emotional Awareness Team Stress Tolerance	Intrapersonal Stress Management	Emotional Self-Awareness Impulse Control

LPI	MBTI		Emergenetics		FIRO-B
Practice	Dimension	Facet	Thinking	Behavioral	Need
All	Extraversion Introversion Sensing Feeling	Expressive Reflective Experiential Empathetic Accepting	Social Analytical	Expressiveness Flexibility	All
Enable Others to Act	Introversion Feeling	Reflective Accepting	Social Analytical	Assertiveness Flexibility	Control Affection
Model the Way Inspire a Shared Vision Challenge the Process	Extraversion Introversion Thinking Feeling	Initiating Expressive Reflective Logical Accommodating	All	All	All
All	Introversion Intuition Thinking Feeling	Reflective Imaginative Logical Empathetic	All	Expressiveness Flexibility	All
Model the Way	Introversion	Reflective	Analytical	Flexibility	Control

(Continued)

Connecting the Exercises with the Assessments (*continued*)

Exercise	Page	EISA	TESI	EQi Composite	EQi Subscale	
5.3 Decision Making, Emotions, and Thinking Styles	91	Decision Making	All	Intrapersonal Interpersonal Adaptability	Self-Regard Emotional Self-Awareness Empathy Social Responsibility Interpersonal Relationships Reality Testing Flexibility Problem Solving	
6.1 Emotional Well-Being	101	Achieving	Team Emotional Awareness Team Stress Tolerance Team Positive Mood	Intrapersonal Stress Management Adaptability General Mood	Self-Regard Emotional Self-Awareness Self-Actualization Impulse Control Reality Testing Optimism Happiness	
6.2 Collaborating	106	Achieving	All	All	Emotional Self-Awareness Assertiveness Empathy Interpersonal Relationships Impulse Control Flexibility Problem Solving Optimism	
6.3 Aligning Your Power	110	Achieving	Team Motivation Team Emotional Awareness Team Conflict Resolution Team Positive Mood	All	Self-Regard Emotional Self-Awareness Self-Actualization Interpersonal Relationships Impulse Control Reality Testing Optimism	

LPI	MBTI		Emergenetics		FIRO-B
Practice	Dimension	Facet	Thinking	Behavioral	Need
Inspire a Shared Vision Enable Others to Act Encourage the Heart	Extraversion Introversion Sensing Intuition Thinking Feeling	Initiating Receiving Expressive Intimate Active Reflective Concrete Conceptual Experiential Logical Empathetic Accepting	All	All	Inclusion Affection
All	Introversion Intuition Thinking Feeling	Reflective Conceptual Reasonable Accepting	Analytical Conceptual Social	Assertiveness Flexibility	All
All	Extraversion Introversion Feeling	Initiating Receiving Expressive Reflective Logical Empathetic Reasonable Accommodating	Social Analytical Conceptual	All	All
Enable Others to Act	Introversion Thinking Feeling	Reflective Logical Empathetic Questioning Accepting	Analytical Conceptual	Flexibility	Control

(Continued)

Exercise	Page	EISA	TESI	EQi	
				Composite	Subscale

7.1 Be a Magnet	117	Influencing	Team Identity
			Team Motivation
			Team Emotional
			    Awareness
				Intrapersonal
				Interpersonal
				Adaptability
					Emotional
					    Self-Awareness
					Empathy
					Reality Testing
					Problem Solving

7.2 Engaged Listening	127	Influencing	Team Motivation
			Team Emotional
			    Awareness
			Team
			    Communication
			Team Conflict
			    Resolution
				All	Emotional
					    Self-Awareness
					Empathy
					Impulse Control
					Flexibility
					Optimism

7.3 Achieve Your G.O.A.L. with Effective Feedback	131	Influencing	Team Motivation
			Team
			    Communication
				Intrapersonal
				Interpersonal
				Adaptability
					Assertiveness
					Interpersonal
					    Relationships
					Problem Solving

8.1 Team Identity Scavenger Hunt	143	Perceiving Influencing	Team Identity	Interpersonal Adaptability	Social Responsibility Interpersonal Relationships Reality Testing
8.2 Walk in My Shoes	149	All	Team Identity	Interpersonal Stress Management Adaptability	Empathy Stress Tolerance Reality Testing Flexibility Problem Solving
8.3 Building Team Values	152	Perceiving Achieving Influencing	Team Identity	Intrapersonal Interpersonal General Mood	Self-Regard Emotional Self-Awareness Self-Actualization Social Responsibility Optimism Happiness

9.1 Success Through Being on Target	159	All	Team Motivation	Intrapersonal
				Interpersonal
					Emotional
					    Self-Awareness
					Empathy
					Interpersonal
					    Relationships

LPI	MBTI		Emergenetics		FIRO-B
Practice	Dimension	Facet	Thinking	Behavioral	Need
All	Introversion Thinking Feeling	Reflective Questioning Empathetic	Social Analytical	Expressiveness Assertiveness	Inclusion Control
All	Extraversion Introversion Sensing Thinking Feeling	Initiating Receiving Expressive Intimate Reflective Experiential Empathetic Questioning	Social Analytical	Expressiveness Flexibility	All
All	Extraversion Feeling	Initiating Expressive Empathetic Accommodating Compassionate	Social Analytical Conceptual	Assertiveness Flexibility	All
Model the Way	Extraversion Perceiving	Initiating Active Emergent	Social	Expressiveness Assertiveness Flexibility	Inclusion
Challenge the Process	Extraversion Sensing Feeling Perceiving	Active Experiential Accommodating Open-Ended Spontaneous	Social	Flexibility	All
Model the Way Inspire a Shared Vision Enable Others to Act Encourage the Heart	Introversion Intuition Feeling	Reflective Abstract Conceptual Accommodating	Conceptual Social	Expressiveness	Inclusion Affection
Enable Others to Act Encourage the Heart	Extraversion Feeling	Expressive Empathetic Accommodating	Social	Expressiveness	Affection

(Continued)

27

Connecting the Exercises with the Assessments (*continued*)

Exercise	Page	EISA	TESI	EQi Composite	EQi Subscale
9.2 Attitude Rules Motivation	162	All	Team Motivation	Intrapersonal Interpersonal General Mood	Emotional Self-Awareness Social Responsibility Happiness Optimism
9.3 Focusing on Inspiration	166	Achieving Influencing	Team Motivation	All	Self-Actualization Interpersonal Relationships Problem Solving Optimism
10.1 Name That Emotion	171	Perceiving Managing	Team Emotional Awareness	Intrapersonal Interpersonal	Emotional Self-Awareness Empathy
10.2 Noticing Emotions	175	All	Team Emotional Awareness	Intrapersonal Interpersonal General Mood	Emotional Self-Awareness Empathy Interpersonal Relationships Happiness
10.3 Paying Attention to Us	179	Perceiving Managing	Team Emotional Awareness	Intrapersonal Interpersonal Adaptability General Mood	Self -Regard Emotional Self-Awareness Assertiveness Empathy Interpersonal Relationships Flexibility Happiness
11.1 Listening with the Ears of Your Heart	185	Perceiving Managing	Team Communication	Interpersonal	Empathy Interpersonal Relationships
11.2 Diversity Mania	191	Managing Influencing	Team Communication	Intrapersonal Interpersonal	Assertiveness Interpersonal Relationships

LPI	MBTI		Emergenetics		FIRO-B
Practice	Dimension	Facet	Thinking	Behavioral	Need
Model the Way Enable Others to Act Encourage the Heart	Extraversion Feeling	Expressive Empathetic	Social	Expressiveness Flexibility	Affection
All	Extraversion Feeling Judging	Initiating Expressive Compassionate Planful	Analytical Conceptual Social	Assertiveness Expressiveness	All
Enable Others to Act Encourage the Heart	Extraversion Feeling	Expressive Empathetic	Social	Expressiveness Flexibility	Affection
Enable Others to Act Encourage the Heart	Extraversion Feeling	Expressive Empathetic Compassionate	Social	Expressiveness Flexibility	Affection
Enable Others to Act Encourage the Heart	Extraversion Introversion Feeling	Initiating Receiving Expressive Intimate Reflective Enthusiastic Quiet Empathetic Accepting	Social	Expressiveness Flexibility	Inclusion Affection
Enable Others to Act	Introversion	Reflective Intimate Quiet	Social	Flexibility	Affection
Enable Others to Act Encourage the Heart	Extraversion	Initiating Gregarious Expressive Enthusiastic	Social	Assertiveness Expressiveness	Inclusion Affection

(Continued)

Connecting the Exercises with the Assessments (*continued*)

Exercise	Page	EISA	TESI	EQi	
				Composite	Subscale
11.3 Turn Off Email!	195	Managing Decision Making	Team Communication	Intrapersonal Interpersonal Stress Management Adaptability	Assertiveness Interpersonal Relationships Stress Tolerance Impulse Control Flexibility
12.1 Work and Play	201	Decision Making Achieving Influencing	Team Stress Tolerance	Intrapersonal Interpersonal Stress Management	Self-Actualization Empathy Interpersonal Relationships Stress Tolerance Happiness
12.2 When the Internet Is Down	204	Managing Decision Making Achieving Influencing	Team Stress Tolerance	All	Emotional Self-Awareness Assertiveness Empathy Social Responsibility Stress Tolerance Impulse Control Reality Testing Flexibility Problem Solving Optimism Happiness
12.3 Energizers and Stress Triggers	208	Perceiving Managing Influencing	Team Stress Tolerance	All	Emotional Self-Awareness Assertiveness Interpersonal Relationships Stress Tolerance Impulse Control Reality Testing Flexibility Problem Solving Optimism
13.1 SWOT Your Team Conflict	215	Decision Making Achieving Influencing	Team Conflict Resolution	Interpersonal Adaptability General Mood	Social Responsibility Reality Testing Problem Solving

LPI	MBTI		Emergenetics		FIRO-B
Practice	Dimension	Facet	Thinking	Behavioral	Need
Challenge the Process Enable Others to Act	Extraversion	Initiating Expressive Gregarious Active	Social	All	Inclusion Affection
All	Extraversion Intuition	Expressive Imaginative	Conceptual Social	Assertiveness Expressiveness	Affection
All	Extraversion Sensing Thinking Feeling Judging Perceiving	Initiating Expressive Active Concrete Realistic Experiential Empathetic Planful Pressure- Prompted Spontaneous Emergent	All	All	All
All	Extraversion Introversion Sensing Intuition Feeling	Initiating Expressive Reflective Concrete Imaginative Empathetic Accepting	Social Analytical	Expressiveness Flexibility	Inclusion Affection
All	Extraversion Intuition Thinking Feeling	Expressive Imaginative Logical Questioning Empathetic Accommodating	Analytical	Assertiveness Expressiveness	Inclusion Control

(Continued)

Exercise	Page	EISA	TESI	EQi	
				Composite	Subscale
13.2 Judging or Open-Minded?	219	All	Team Conflict Resolution	All	Emotional Self-Awareness Empathy Interpersonal Relationships Impulse Control Reality Testing Flexibility Happiness
13.3 To Confront or Not to Confront	223	All	Team Conflict Resolution	Intrapersonal Interpersonal Stress Management Adaptability	Assertiveness Interpersonal Relationships Stress Tolerance Impulse Control Problem Solving
14.1 Cultural Fest	231	All	Team Positive Mood	Intrapersonal Interpersonal Adaptability General Mood	Self-Regard Emotional Self-Awareness Empathy Interpersonal Relationships Flexibility Optimism Happiness
14.2 Recognition Cubes	234	Perceiving Managing Influencing	Team Positive Mood	Intrapersonal Interpersonal General Mood	Emotional Self-Awareness Assertiveness Interpersonal Relationships Optimism Happiness
14.3 Rounds of Appreciation	237	Perceiving Managing Influencing	Team Positive Mood	Intrapersonal Interpersonal General Mood	Emotional Self-Awareness Assertiveness Interpersonal Relationships Optimism Happiness

LPI	MBTI		Emergenetics		FIRO-B
Practice	Dimension	Facet	Thinking	Behavioral	Need

Model the Way
Challenge the
   Process
Enable Others
   to Act
	Introversion
	Thinking
	Feeling
		Reflective
		Quiet
		Accepting
		Empathetic
		Compassionate
			Social
			Analytical
				Flexibility	Control
					Affection

Model the Way
Inspire a Shared
   Vision
Challenge the
   Process
Enable Others
   to Act
	Extraversion
	Introversion
	Thinking
	Feeling
		Initiating
		Receiving
		Expressive
		Reflective
		Empathetic
		Reasonable
		Questioning
		Accommodating
		Accepting
			Social
			Analytical
				All	Inclusion
					Control

Enable Others
   to Act
Encourage the
   Heart
	Extraversion
	Introversion
	Sensing
	Intuition
	Feeling
	Judging
	Perceiving
		Initiating
		Receiving
		Expressive
		Active
		Reflective
		Experiential
		Imaginative
		Empathetic
		Accepting
		Planful
		Spontaneous
			Social
			Conceptual
				Expressiveness
				Flexibility
					Affection

Encourage the Heart	Extraversion Introversion Feeling	Initiating Receiving Expressive Reflective Empathetic Accepting	Social	Expressiveness	Affection
Encourage the Heart	Extraversion Introversion Feeling	Initiating Receiving Expressive Reflective Empathetic Accepting	Social	Expressiveness	Affection

Exercises to Use in Developing Emotionally Intelligent Leaders and Individuals, Organized in the Five Categories of the EISA

Skill	Time to Complete Exercise
Perceiving	
3.1 Emotional Congruence	25 to 35 minutes
3.2 Emotions Bingo	25 to 40 minutes
3.3 Acknowledging Ambivalence	40 to 50 minutes
Managing	
4.1 Success in Managing Emotions	25 to 50 minutes
4.2 From Emotional Intensity to Curiosity	30 minutes
4.3 The Essential Conversation	35 to 60 minutes
Decision Making	
5.1 Emotions Inform Decisions	30 minutes
5.2 Who's In Control—You or Your Impulses? Developing Self-Mastery	30 to 40 minutes
5.3 Decision Making, Emotions, and Thinking Styles	40 to 45 minutes
Achieving	
6.1 Emotional Well-Being	25 to 40 minutes
6.2 Collaborating	35 minutes
6.3 Aligning Your Power	25 to 35 minutes
Influencing	
7.1 Be a Magnet	10 to 20 minutes
7.2 Engaged Listening	25 minutes
7.3 Achieve Your G.O.A.L. with Effective Feedback	50 minutes

CHAPTER 3

Perceiving*

*"The ability to accurately recognize, attend
to, and understand emotion."*

This EISA factor measures your ability to:

- Understand your own emotions
- Stay attuned to the emotions of others
- Demonstrate empathy
- Differentiate between emotions

Perceiving is the first of the five EISA emotional intelligence competencies. Underlying all other competencies, perceiving is a person's awareness of his or her own emotions, and a recognition and understanding of the emotions of others.

---

*The introductory material in this section is derived from S. Stein, D. Mann, P. Papadogiannis, and W. Gordon (2010), *The Emotional Intelligence Skills Assessment (EISA) Facilitators' Guide*. San Francisco, CA: Pfeiffer.

People with strong perceiving skills have a vocabulary for emotions that goes beyond happy, mad, sad, and glad. They appreciate that each individual has a unique emotional response to any situation. Those who are skilled in perceiving are often called intuitive, authentic, empathic, predictable, insightful, visionary, or motivating, because of their ability to attend to their own and others' emotions.

Skilled perceivers can confidently answer questions regarding what they are feeling, what brings them joy, and what triggers their anger. They are less likely to trigger a strong negative emotional response in someone else because a skilled perceiver would use his or her perceiving skills to anticipate and plan for how another person might respond to difficult information. Skilled perceivers are also more likely to effectively communicate with and influence others, because they use their perceiving skills to best tailor their approach to their audience.

Those who are less skilled at perceiving may find others unpredictable and be frustrated to learn that others view them the same way. They might have a hard time recognizing and interpreting non-verbal communications—including body language and tone of voice—which exacerbates their difficulties in relationships because nonverbal communications convey interpersonal information in a powerful way. Some less-skilled perceivers rely so much on their rational, intellectual, and analytical abilities that they find it hard to lead others through emotionally intense times such as organizational change. Their focus on thoughts and words rather than emotions and nonverbal cues forces them to miss vital information.

Perceiving is an essential skill for maintaining successful relationships with others, and one that can be improved throughout one's lifetime. Following are three exercises for building the skill of perceiving.

EXERCISE 3.1. EMOTIONAL CONGRUENCE

Purpose

To expand your clients' skills in perceiving their own emotions, which leads to more accurate verbal and nonverbal communications.

Thumbnail

25 to 35 minutes

Clients reflect on their own communications and, guided through several specific steps, evaluate how effective they were at perceiving and communicating their emotions. They then practice these skills either immediately afterward (in pairs) or as homework for later follow-up.

Outcomes

Clients will build reflective awareness of the accuracy of how well they perceive their own emotions and how well they communicate those emotions to others. They will then learn to apply this awareness in order to improve their skills in future communications.

Audience

- Individuals in coaching session or group training
- Intact teams
- Individual team members desiring to build skills to take back to the team
- Team leaders

Facilitator Competencies

 Moderate

Materials

- Pens
- Emotional Congruence Handout

Time Matrix

Activity	Estimated Time
Discuss emotional congruence	5 minutes
Distribute Emotional Congruence Handout; list ten past events that included emotional message and follow steps on handout	10 to 15 minutes
Practice and debrief, either in pairs or as homework to debrief at next session	10 to 15 minutes
Total Time	**25 to 35 minutes**

Instructions

1. Discuss the power of emotional perception. When one understands how he or she feels and how those emotions are being demonstrated, the ability to communicate effectively is greatly expanded. Additionally, this awareness creates a congruent and powerful communication to others who are then much more capable of accurately perceiving the emotional message intended. If a colleague says he is "Just fine, thank you" in a tight voice with a grumpy look on his face, no one is fooled into thinking things are fine. He's giving mixed messages that hurt the communication. Nonverbal messages are accepted as much more accurate than verbal messages, so the grumpy face will be believed. With emotional congruence underlying the message, the speaker presents a message he or she is aware of and intends to communicate so the verbal and nonverbal signals match. This is a winning proposition for effective communication. Having presented this information, invite discussion.

2. Distribute a copy of the Emotional Congruence Handout. Ask your coaching client or the group participants to quickly list ten events that occurred in the last week in which their communication included an emotional message. It can be anything from, "Yes, I'd love an ice cream cone!" to telling someone about a serious concern. Just make the list.

3. Direct them to:
   - Rate each item on a scale of 1 to 10 regarding how well they believe they communicated the whole message—content and emotions.
   - List what emotions were reflected and how they were conveyed verbally and nonverbally.
   - Rate how effective the response was.
   - State whether they felt personally satisfied about the conclusion to the interaction.

   This first step, described above, is focused on building reflective awareness of the accuracy of how well individuals perceive their own emotions and how well they communicate those emotions. Emphasize that mastery comes from practice, and encourage continued self awareness.

4. There is a choice for the second step to the exercise.
   - If you are coaching or training an individual or group that will be back for another session, give them homework to write a summary of an emotional communication every evening for the next week and bring it back. Be sure to ask to review the homework at the next session and discuss it.
   - If this is a one-time training with a group, organize them in pairs to practice by exchanging a new message and then evaluating their success by using the steps in the handout. In the pairs Person A will speak first for one or two minutes, then Person B will give his or her message. Finally, both should take two minutes to debrief.

Tip

Look for ways to create follow-up to this exercise as practice that will build heightened awareness and bring the rewards of congruence between the speaker and those receiving the message.

EMOTIONAL CONGRUENCE HANDOUT

Instructions:

1. In the chart below, list ten events that occurred in the last week in which your communication included an emotional message.
2. Rate each item on a scale of 1 to 10 regarding how well you believe you communicated the whole message—content and emotions.
3. List what emotions were reflected and how they were conveyed verbally and nonverbally.
4. List how effective the response was.
5. Did you feel personally satisfied about the conclusion to the interaction?
6. What could you have said or done to increase your level of satisfaction?

Ten Events	Rate effectiveness from 1 to 10	Emotions reflected and how conveyed verbally and nonverbally	Effective?	Was I satisfied?
1				
2				
3				
4				
5				
6				
7				
8				
9				
10				
Other reflections:				

EXERCISE 3.2. EMOTIONS BINGO

Purpose

To build clients' vocabulary of words that communicate emotions and to build their understanding of how using those words affects their ability to perceive emotions and communicate effectively.

Thumbnail

25 to 40 minutes

Individual clients or small groups of clients are given a bingo chart and encouraged to fill in the blanks by generating as many emotions words as possible in a short period of time. They then build a story with their words and discuss how well the emotional content is communicated with those words.

Outcomes

Clients will build emotional vocabulary and expand their awareness and skills in using emotion words. They will also expand their ability to perceive their own emotions and to more accurately communicate those emotions to others.

Audience

- Individuals in coaching session or group training
- Intact teams
- Individual team members desiring to build skills to take back to the team
- Team leaders

Facilitator Competencies

 Easy to Moderate

Materials

- Pens
- Timer or clock

- An Emotions Bingo Handout for each participant or group
- A copy of the Emotions Bingo Handout—Facilitator Copy for reference
- A prize

Time Matrix

Activity	Estimated Time
Explain about building emotional vocabulary and the value to improving perceptions	5 minutes
Divide into groups; ask them to fill in the Emotions Bingo Handout. Groups read their words and a prize is given to winner	5 to 10 minutes
Groups fill in any blank categories	5 minutes
Each group writes a story	5 to 10 minutes
Each group reads its story and the full group debriefs	5 to 10 minutes
Total Time	**25 to 40 minutes**

Instructions

1. Explain that this is an opportunity for your participants to play, to build their vocabulary of words that communicate emotions, and then to apply those words to an event in their lives. This exercise is designed to build their ability to perceive their own emotions accurately and to help others perceive their emotions by using effective emotional descriptors.

2. Divide the training group or team into small groups of four or five or a number that fits your group size. Give each small group one copy of the Emotions Bingo Handout and tell them they have five minutes to work together to fill in as many words as they can. Note the categories on the bingo chart are the letters E M O T E and that they have the challenge of identifying five emotion words that begin with each letter. At the end of five minutes call time. Ask each group to report how many words they identified and to read the words. Give a prize to the group that has the most words on their bingo chart. Be prepared with extra prizes in case there is a tie.

3. Help the groups fill in any blank spaces so that the chart is completely filled. They can write in words generated by other groups; if more are needed you can give them ideas. A separate handout is provided as a guide for you, and a comprehensive list of emotions can be found in the Appendix.

4. Ask each group to now write a story about a real event that occurred. The story can be about an event that happened to one person or to the entire group. Each story should use at least ten emotion words, with not more than two emotion words per sentence.

5. Read the stories out loud to everyone and debrief. As they consider each story, ask questions such as:
   - Did the group story identify the emotions you feel will best help all those involved perceive and understand the emotions that are involved in the story?
   - What other emotions would you add?
   - What ideas do you have to improve the use of recognizing and demonstrating emotions to support effective interaction?

Tip

Guide the groups to take the stories seriously because this is a valuable opportunity to learn how to effectively build perception of emotional messages.

This group exercise can be adapted easily to work with an individual coachee.

EMOTIONS BINGO HANDOUT

Instructions: Fill in as many emotions words as you can that begin with the letter at the top of the column. You have five minutes.

E	M	O	T	E

EMOTIONS BINGO HANDOUT—
FACILITATOR COPY

Instructions: Fill in as many emotions words as you can that begin with the letter at the top of the column. You have five minutes.

E	M	O	T	E
Energized	Mischievous	Obligated	Tickled	Elated
Empathetic	Motivated	Optimistic	Terrified	Eager
Enthusiastic	Miserable	Offended	Tormented	Exasperated
Envious	Merry	Overwhelmed	Tenacious	Excited
Embarrassed	Misunderstood	Over the moon	Thoughtful	Ecstatic

EXERCISE 3.3. ACKNOWLEDGING AMBIVALENCE

Purpose

To increase clients' ability to perceive and accept conflicting feelings that prevent them and others from gaining clarity regarding their emotions and behaviors.

Thumbnail

40 to 50 minutes

Clients consider a situation in which they may be experiencing conflicting feelings, identify those feelings, and explore the benefits and consequences of attempting to resolve the conflict.

Outcomes

Clients will learn to recognize when they are experiencing ambivalent feelings, to identify these feelings, and to leverage this knowledge to improve their ability to accurately perceive and explore a variety of emotions in themselves and others. This will help them more effectively guide their own behavior and perceive and respond to others' confusing behavior.

Audience

- Individuals in coaching session or group training
- Intact teams
- Individual team members desiring to build skills to take back to the team
- Team leaders

Facilitator Competencies

 Moderate to Advanced

Materials

- Pens
- Acknowledging Ambivalence Handout

Time Matrix

Activity	Estimated Time
Introduce the concept of ambivalence and distribute handout	5 minutes
Clients complete handout	15 to 20 minutes
Provide examples and discuss as a group	15 to 20 minutes
Review and summarize	5 minutes
Total Time	**40 to 50 minutes**

Instructions

1. Introduce the concept of ambivalence by stating that it is a myth that people can only experience one emotion at a time. Often when people are confused, paralyzed in indecision, lacking motivation, slow to act, or having a hard time perceiving their own or others' emotions, it is not because they don't have strong feelings about something, but because they are ambivalent. They have strong conflicting feelings that are pulling them simultaneously toward and away from an idea, person, or behavior. Because people can feel overwhelmed with the strength of the conflicting emotions or can experience discomfort with the internal conflict those emotions create, they may try to ignore or push one emotion out of the way in an attempt to favor the other. But this can block their ability to accurately understand and respond to the breadth of emotional feedback available.

2. Have your clients turn to the Acknowledging Ambivalence Handout. Ask them to consider a current situation in which they feel some discomfort, such as feeling confused, unmotivated, indecisive, or frustrated. Give them a few minutes to identify this situation and summarize it in one or two sentences on the handout. Assure them of confidentiality. They will keep their handouts and, while they will be debriefing as a group afterward, no one will be required to share any information he or she does not wish to share. This exercise is for their personal exploration.

3. Next, ask them to review the list of emotions in Step 2 on the handout. Have them consider their situations and circle the word that best describes one of their feelings regarding this situation. If none of the listed emotions is accurate for them, instruct them to write down the word that best describes that feeling in the space below. Then ask them to fill in Step 3 by writing a few sentences to describe the circumstances that might be contributing to their feeling this emotion in this situation. As they write, have them also identify any conflicting emotions they have about the situation. For example, if they chose a difficult emotion (from the column on the left), ask them to consider whether they might also be experiencing a more positive emotion about a different aspect of the same situation. Have them choose a word in the column opposite the first word they chose or write down an emotion that conflicts with the first word they chose.

4. In Step 4 ask them to write a few sentences to describe the circumstances that might be contributing to their feeling different emotions in this situation. Give them time to complete the handout (approximately fifteen additional minutes).

5. Once everyone has finished, debrief by inviting comments from those who would like to speak. Be prepared with examples of relevant situations that everyone can discuss. Possible situations might include:

- I should be so excited about this new opportunity; why am I not acting on it?
- I want to take on new responsibilities, but am struggling because it means I will have to delegate responsibilities that bring satisfaction and reward.
- I want to have a better relationship with a co-worker, but also feel competitive toward this person because we are peers wanting the same promotion.
- I want to be more social with colleagues, but I am introverted and those settings drain me.
- I find myself saying one thing and acting in another way and don't know why.

6. Choose one situation and encourage the group to explore possible responses to the remaining questions. For example, they may decide to explore the situation of hiring a new person. They may be feeling

pessimistic regarding having no time to train the new person; having fewer financial resources for other needs because of this new person's salary; wondering whether the interview process wasn't thorough enough to find the perfect candidate; and thinking the new person's personality style may conflict with other team members. On the other hand, they may be feeling optimistic that they are getting new talent; that they will eventually be relieved of some of their own workload; and that the team may really grow with this new person's influence and skills.

7. Help them understand that sometimes just recognizing and identifying the conflicting feelings can be enough to gain clarity and move them toward resolution. However, this is not always the case, so help them consider how they can use their positive feelings to work through the more challenging ones and resolve at least some of their internal conflict. For example, how can they leverage their strong optimism regarding one aspect to alleviate their pessimism regarding another? Ask them to consider whether it is even possible or desirable to resolve the conflict between these two emotions. While most people want to resolve any kind of emotional conflict to reach the relief of absolute clarity, it may not be possible, or even desirable, to do so. You might ask:

   • How might the two emotions actually work together to help them be more successful?

   • How does the more uncomfortable emotion serve them? For example, can pessimism (or doubt) keep them from barreling full force down a path that requires a more measured pace?

   • Can fear motivate them to prepare more fully for an important interaction?

   Guide them to use the positive emotions and energy they provide while also paying heed to the concerns the other emotions raise.

8. As a part of the conclusion ask, "How will your awareness of the reality of conflicting emotions help you more accurately perceive your own, and others', emotions in the future?" After the group shares their comments, express the hope that this exercise has helped them let go of the expectation that they and others experience only one emotion at a time. Acknowledge that they have started building skills in perceiving and accepting ambivalence in themselves and others, which will help them

more effectively guide their own behavior and more appropriately perceive and respond to others' confusing behavior.

9. *Optional Stretch Goal:* There are many ways people communicate ambivalence. Ask for examples of how verbal and nonverbal behaviors can contradict each other. You may need to remind the group that vocal qualities such as speed and inflection, not just choice of words, are powerful communicators as well.

Tip

This exercise ties in with many of the concepts discussed in the conflict resolution exercises you will find in Part Three, as learning to perceive and accept conflict within ourselves also builds skills in dealing with interpersonal conflict.

ACKNOWLEDGING AMBIVALENCE
HANDOUT

Instructions:

1. Consider a current situation in which you are feeling some discomfort and would like to gain more clarity. This could be a situation in which you may be feeling confused, unmotivated, indecisive, or frustrated.

2. As you reflect on this situation, review the following list of emotions. Do any of them describe at least one of your feelings about this situation? If so, circle the word. If not, write down any emotion that comes to mind in the space below.

Doubtful	Confident
Impatient	Patient
Fearful	Courageous
Anxious	Trusting
Pessimistic	Optimistic
Annoyed	Amused
Uncertain	Certain
Reluctant	Motivated
Inadequate	Competent

3. Describe your feelings in more detail and, while you do so, also notice conflicting emotions you experience when you think of this situation. For example, if you chose a more difficult emotion (from the column on the left), consider that you might also be experiencing a more positive emotion about a different aspect of this same situation. Choose one of the words in the column on the right that describes this more positive emotion, or write down your own word that describes the conflicting emotion.

4. What circumstances might be contributing to you feeling these different ways?

5. Now consider these two conflicting emotions. How does it feel to recognize that you might have strong conflicting feelings about this same situation?

6. Is it possible to resolve the conflict between these two emotions? Is one more powerful than the other? For example, can you leverage your strong confidence in one aspect to alleviate your doubt in another?

7. Is it desirable to resolve the conflict between these two emotions? How might it help or hurt you to do so? How might the tension between these conflicting emotions serve you?

8. How do your behaviors demonstrate that you are conflicted? For example, do you say one thing and do another?

9. When have you suspected ambivalence in another person? Do you have a sense of what those emotions are? How did it affect your interactions?

CHAPTER 4

Managing*

"The ability to effectively manage, control, and express emotions."

This EISA factor measures your ability to:

- Effectively manage emotions
- Effectively control emotions
- Appropriately express emotions

While perceiving is recognizing and understanding emotions, managing emotions entails handling emotions and is demonstrated by how those emotions are reflected in a person's behaviors.

People skilled at managing emotions are calm in challenging situations, not thrown off-balance by their own or others' emotions. They express themselves well, listen attentively,

---

*The introductory material in this section is derived from S. Stein, D. Mann, P. Papadogiannis, and W. Gordon (2010), *The Emotional Intelligence Skills Assessment (EISA) Facilitators' Guide*. San Francisco, CA: Pfeiffer.

know how to say no effectively, and cope with stress without negatively impacting relationships or emotional or physical health. They are able to change the intensity of their emotions so that they are not overwhelming to others, to accept conflict as an opportunity to improve a situation, and to plan accordingly if they recognize that a situation might trigger intense emotions.

Those less skilled at managing might be seen as impulsive, aggressive or timid, anxious, and stressed. They might interrupt frequently, not pay attention, rush to solutions before considering important information, or have physical responses to stress such as headaches, stomach aches, or blurred vision. They are uncomfortable in situations in which people are expressing their emotions, are surprised by their own emotional reactions to a seemingly minor event, and might struggle to express their emotional experience to others. They might have made impulsive decisions that had a negative life impact, and they are less likely to build solid rapport and develop meaningful relationships with others.

Managing emotions is one of the most critical skills needed for effective social interactions. The following three exercises are for building the skill of managing.

EXERCISE 4.1. SUCCESS IN MANAGING EMOTIONS

Purpose

To develop clients' skills in managing their own emotions.

Thumbnail

25 to 50 minutes

Clients write about and then discuss (in pairs or individually with their coach) one successful and one unsuccessful past event in their lives. They explore how emotions were felt and expressed in both scenarios and identify effective managing behaviors that they then utilize in planning for future scenarios.

Outcomes

Through reviewing examples of prior emotional management, clients identify more effective managing behaviors and apply those learnings to making better decisions about expressing their emotions in the future.

Audience

- Individuals in coaching session or group training
- Intact teams
- Individual team members desiring to build skills to take back to the team
- Team leaders

Facilitator Competencies

 Moderate to Advanced

Materials

- Pens and paper
- Flip-chart paper, easel, and markers
- Success in Managing Emotions Handout

Time Matrix

Exercise	Estimated Time
Discuss meaning and purpose of emotional management	5 minutes
Distribute and complete the Success in Managing Emotions Handout	5 to 10 minutes
Discuss the positive and negative scenarios and the emotions present for each	10 to 20 minutes
Identify a possible future scenario and strategize successful emotional management	5 to 15 minutes
Total Time	**25 to 50 minutes**

Instructions

1. Discuss the purpose and intent of emotional management. First ask your clients to describe what emotional management means. Ask for specifics and write the key points down so all can see them. If you are working with an individual, write the notes on a piece of paper; if you are working with a group, use a whiteboard or flip chart. Then discuss emotional management from your perspective. Emphasize that it includes these categories as identified in the EISA:
   - Effectively managing your own emotions
   - Effectively controlling your own emotions
   - Appropriately expressing your emotions
2. Distribute the Success in Managing Emotions Handout, pens, and extra paper. Ask each individual to take ten minutes to describe two scenarios in which they were involved. Guide them to include specific emotions and actions for each scenario. Discuss the importance of writing about two very different situations—one that was handled successfully, and one that was quite the opposite, a challenge or even what might feel like a failure. Point out the importance of writing down every emotional word that comes to mind as they think about the scenarios. They are not to fill in the third scenario in the handout at this time.

Developing Emotional and Social Intelligence

3. After they have completed their scenarios, and without judgment regarding the fortunate or unfortunate scenario, discuss the observations gained from what is written. If it's an individual coaching session, ask your client to discuss the scenarios. If you are working with a group or team, ask them to form pairs and discuss the results. Instruct them to start with the difficult outcome scenario, and then move to the positive outcome scenario. During the discussion, guide the clients to connect their emotions with a reason for the emotion. Ask them to discuss the progression of emotions experienced throughout the events as reflected by their responses to this sentence in the handout:

When _____ occurred, I felt _____ because _____.

Also suggest they discuss what they noticed in their body—stress, tension, relaxation—as emotions also show up in the body, which they may notice first.

4. Now that they have looked at both a situation that worked and one that did not, ask your clients to think more about how their management of the emotions affected the outcome. With these new insights, have them consider a third scenario, a situation some time in the future in which they can imagine managing their emotions differently in order to gain a better outcome. Give them five minutes to complete this section of the handout. Guide them to make the sample specific, to see, feel, hear and touch real parts of what is happening in the scenario and to identify the accompanying emotions. Discuss these possibilities and focus on improved management of emotions in the new scenario. Utilize the strengths from the scenario that worked, while being aware of the challenges that can arise as identified in the unsuccessful scenario.

Tip

The purpose of this exercise is to focus on how clients can make better choices in the future. Therefore, explore how they can continue this process to make better decisions based on what they are learning in the writing and discussions.

SUCCESS IN MANAGING EMOTIONS HANDOUT

Instructions: Write about two very different situations in which you have been involved—one handled successfully and one that was quite the opposite, a challenge or even what might feel like a failure. As you are writing, it is important that you write down every emotional word that comes to mind as you think about the scenarios.

Scenario One—Not So Successful

1. Write a brief description of an event in which you were involved when you were not pleased with how you participated in the process or the solution. Write down every emotional word that comes to mind as a part of the process. You might write the words as a list or include them in the scenario. Consider any feelings you felt in your body, stress or tension, for example, as emotions can also be expressed and first noticed as a physical sensation.

2. Unpack the emotions from this scenario. Notice what occurred specifically and complete at least three of the sentences below. Consider the developing experience and expression of your emotions. Thus, the first sentence can be about how you first felt, the second about an emotion as events evolved, and the third sentence about how you felt at the conclusion:

- When _____ occurred, I felt _____ because _____.

- When _____ occurred, I felt _____ because _____.

- When _____ occurred, I felt _____ because _____.

Scenario Two—Successful

1. Write a brief description of an event in which you were involved when you were pleased with how you participated in the process or the solution. Write down every emotional word that comes to mind as a part of the process. You might write the words as a list or include them in the scenario. Consider any feelings you felt in your body, stress or tension, for example, as emotions can also be expressed and first noticed as a physical sensation.

2. Unpack the emotions from this scenario. Notice what occurred specifically and complete at least three of the sentences below. Consider the developing experience and expression of your emotions. Thus, the first sentence can be about how you first felt, the second about an emotion as events evolved, and the third sentence about how you felt at the conclusion:

- When _____ occurred, I felt _____ because _____.

- When _____ occurred, I felt _____ because _____.

- When _____ occurred, I felt _____ because _____.

Scenario Three—Future Success

Write a description of a future event in which you might be involved where you will be successful in your participation in the process and in the solution. See, feel, hear, and touch real parts of what is happening in the scenario and identify the accompanying emotions. Utilize the strengths from the scenario that worked, while being aware of the challenges that can arise as identified in the unsuccessful scenario.

EXERCISE 4.2. FROM EMOTIONAL INTENSITY TO CURIOSITY

Purpose

To provide a process that will help individuals manage intense emotions so that they can respond to stressful situations in a more emotionally effective way.

Thumbnail

30 minutes

Clients identify a stressful situation and practice shifting away from intense blaming and judgmental language to more neutral, curious language.

Outcomes

Clients will gain expertise in managing intense emotions that arise in stressful situations. This will lead to less defensiveness and more productive relationships with others, better solutions, and an improved outlook and emotional experience.

Audience

- Individuals in coaching session or group training
- Individual team members desiring to build skills to take back to the team
- Team leaders

Facilitator Competencies

 Moderate

Materials

- Pens
- From Emotional Intensity to Curiosity Handout

Time Matrix

Exercise	Estimated Time
Introduce the topic of emotional intensity and review handout	5 minutes
Clients identify a challenging situation to explore	5 minutes
Clients develop questions that will lead them away from emotional intensity toward a more curious approach	10 minutes
Debrief and plan for future implementation	10 minutes
Total Time	**30 minutes**

Instructions

1. Explain that people often make stressful situations even worse because they increase, rather than reduce, the emotional intensity of their responses. With any situation, individuals can choose how much they care about it, evaluate it, and, ultimately, manage their emotional response to the situation. The more they care about something, the more likely they are to respond intensely. That intensity can make it harder to manage emotions, gain perspective, and explore options. Strong emotions may drive individuals to jump in impulsively and try to solve a problem before fully exploring the situation and the possible options. This disrupts the balance people strive for in themselves and in their relationships.

2. Have your clients turn to the handout. The image indicates the balance of emotional responses to situations in peoples' lives. The left section represents situations in which individuals are not that invested in the outcome, that is, they do not have a strong opinion regarding what should happen. The right section indicates those situations in which they are very invested in the outcome; they care a great deal about what happens. The center section represents the ability to manage each emotional situation in a balanced way: attending to emotions, but not allowing them to control or overwhelm self or others.

3. Work with your client one-on-one if this is an individual session; if it is a group have them form pairs and conduct the following discussions. Ask your clients to:

- First, identify a current (recent past or upcoming) situation in which they feel an intensity that is creating additional stress or apprehension. Explain that this could be a work situation that triggers feelings of anger, frustration, pressure, or annoyance with a peer, boss, or subordinate, or it could be a situation in their personal lives that is not going as well as it could be.

- Second, identify those aspects of the situation that might fall on either end of the spectrum and write those down in the corresponding areas. To help your clients evaluate the situation, ask questions such as: "What do you care about?" "What is not that important?" Ask them to also describe their current emotions regarding those aspects of the situation that fall in the third column. These are often emotions that involve some kind of evaluation or judgment of self or of another person—anger, fear, or frustration. Or the emotions could be intense desire or pride, such as being so proud of an idea that no additional input from others is welcome.

- Third, choose one of those emotions or situations under High Intensity and consider what emotions might become more manageable if they shifted into the middle range of curiosity rather than the extremes of judgment or blame. For example, instead of saying, "This is WRONG!" say, "Isn't it interesting that I feel so strongly about this. I wonder why this is so important to me" or "I'm curious about his strong reaction to what I said. I was only offering my input, but perhaps he thought I was attacking him." Ask them to write these ideas in the middle column. You take them to the middle column last, as you are helping them become calmer and more thoughtful about their emotional engagement.

4. Debrief the exercise with the clients. Possible questions might include:

- Did you notice a shift in your emotions when you started using less judgmental language by working in the middle column and becoming curious?

- What patterns have you noticed regarding types of situations in which you are more likely to feel intense emotions?

- How might you benefit in those situations if you lessened the intensity of your response?
- When you consider the week ahead, what potential situations might trigger intense emotions for you? How might you approach those situations in a curious rather than judgmental way?
- How will you know you're successful?

Tip

This can work in every area of your clients' lives. Whenever an intense emotional response is triggered, your clients can find a word or phrase that helps lead them to movement more toward the middle. Suggest that they start developing a list of the words and phrases that most quickly shift them into curiosity.

FROM EMOTIONAL INTENSITY
TO CURIOSITY HANDOUT

1. Briefly describe the current intense situation

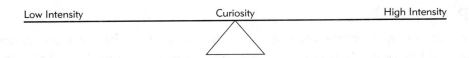

Low Intensity   Curiosity   High Intensity

2. For the current intense situation fill in aspects and associated emotions of this situation:

Answer First	Answer Last	Answer Second
I am not that invested in	I am curious	I am very invested in
When I am not that invested in the outcome, I might:	When I'm curious I might:	When I am very invested in the outcome, I might:

Developing Emotional and Social Intelligence

Examples of positive responses:	**Examples of positive responses**	**Example of positive responses:**
Be willing to let others decide	I wonder about . . .	Be committed and willing to work hard
Help develop and encourage others to succeed at it	I'm surprised. . .	**Examples of less effective responses:**
Examples of less effective responses:	I feel more engaged, present, interested, and thoughtful	Be stubborn, judgmental, irrational
Stop listening		Feel emotionally overwhelmed
Walk away		Feel powerless if I don't get what I want
Become distracted		

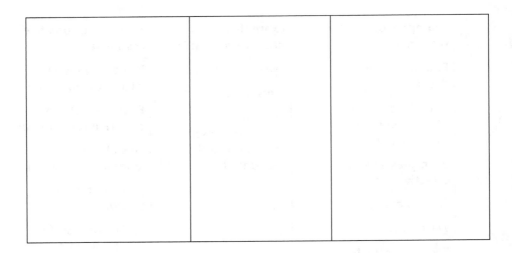

3. Now choose one of the High Intensity emotions above that might become more manageable if you shifted it more toward Curiosity, which is in the middle of the table above. Write about your curiosity. For example, if you are feeling intense anger about a situation, what would happen if you instead had curiosity about your anger or about the situation that triggered it?

Developing Emotional and Social Intelligence

EXERCISE 4.3. THE ESSENTIAL CONVERSATION

Purpose

To help clients gain skills for managing their own and others' emotions in order to create an effective relationship with their bosses. This exercise is written for the employee-boss relationship, but can be modified to apply to any other important relationship.

Thumbnail

35 to 60 minutes, plus conversation with boss and then follow-up conversation to debrief

From the perspective of the employee, clients reflect on past employee-boss experiences, identify those elements that enhance and discourage effective supervisory relationships, and explore their emotional responses to these positive and negative elements. A handout helps clients evaluate their level of satisfaction with their current bosses. They then plan for, role play, and conduct discussions with their bosses, focusing on ways to improve their relationships while also successfully managing their emotions during the interactions.

Outcomes

Clients will develop successful relationships with their bosses by learning to effectively manage emotions during critical conversations about how to best work together. This will also increase positive emotions that result for all parties when mutual expectations are shared and fulfilled, which will lead to an even more rewarding employee-boss relationship.

Audience

- Individuals in coaching session or group training
- Individual team members desiring to build skills to take back to the team
- Team leaders

Facilitator Competencies

Moderate

Materials

- Pens
- Paper
- The Essential Conversation Handout

Time Matrix

Exercise	Estimated Time
Introduce the importance of employee-boss relationship and the role emotions play	5 minutes
Discuss a positive and a negative relationship with a boss	5 to 10 minutes
Clients complete handout, rate relationship with current boss	5 minutes
Discuss the ratings; identify strengths and areas for improvement in relationship	10 to 20 minutes
Role play upcoming meeting with boss, explore emotions, then clients schedule with boss	10 to 20 minutes
After meetings with boss, follow up to debrief	Varies, depending on depth of follow-up conversation
Total Time	**35 to 60 minutes, plus conversation with the boss and debriefing afterward**

Instructions

1. Introduce this exercise by explaining that an effective employee-boss relationship is critical to creating and sustaining a positive work environment. This relationship is impacted by a wide variety of emotions that can be experienced when employees and bosses interact. By intentionally managing the emotions arising in this relationship, clients increase the probability of effective interactions with their bosses and experience an increase in job satisfaction and goal achievement.

2. If you are in an individual coaching session, work with your client on all the steps in this exercise. If you are working with a group, ask group

members to form pairs to conduct the dialogue and role play. Explore your clients' past experiences with bosses by asking them to respond to the following questions. They may wish to record on paper the characteristics, emotions, and patterns identified.

- What characteristics describe the most positive employee-boss relationship(s) you have experienced? What emotions can be identified as a result of this positive relationship? Both your emotions and the emotions of your boss.
- What characteristics describe the most negative employee-boss relationship that you have experienced?
- What emotions can be identified as a result of this negative relationship, both your emotions and the emotions of your boss?
- What patterns do you recognize?

3. Now ask them to rate their current boss relationships by responding to the questions in The Essential Conversation Handout. The instructions are as follows: On a 1 to 5 scale (1 = Poor and 5 = Excellent), rate the following relationship characteristics with your current boss:

- We communicate frequently.
- We communicate about the right things.
- We have a positive relationship.
- My boss recognizes me for my efforts.
- We understand each other.
- My boss utilizes my strengths.
- My boss gives me opportunities to grow and develop.
- My boss and I deal with conflict effectively.

4. Ask everyone to review each of the ratings with you if in a coaching relationship or with his or her partner if you are working with a group. If a rating is 4 or 5, ask about the favorable context and positive emotions that are behind these ratings. If a rating is lower than 4, ask what would be one or two small changes that would make the relationship stronger and more satisfying.

5. Based on this discussion, ask the clients to identify several areas of strength that exist in this relationship with their boss. Then ask for several areas in which improvement is possible.

6. Encourage the clients to take responsibility for managing parts of this relationship by setting up a conversation with the boss. Too often,

employees sit with frustration and despair waiting for the boss to initiate a conversation about how to work together. The employee can greatly benefit by starting this conversation, and the boss frequently appreciates the initiative. The depth of conversation will be based on the type of relationship the client and boss currently share, but in general, instruct your clients to ask the boss for approximately fifteen to twenty minutes of time to clarify what is already working in how they work together and to mutually discover ways in which the relationship could be enhanced.

7. Using the results of The Essential Conversation Handout, guide the clients in setting the content, goals, and tone for this conversation. Help them answer the question, "What do I need in this relationship to be more successful and feel more satisfied?"

8. Explore with your clients how to manage their emotions and expectations during the meeting. Ask them to role play the upcoming conversation and discuss immediately after the role play any emotions the clients experienced. For example, they may say during the role play, "I really appreciate the training opportunities you have given me in project management and time management classes. This knowledge helps me manage my workload more efficiently. I have noticed on several occasions, though, that you seemed frustrated with my reports. I'm unclear as to what you wanted from me that would provide more value to you. Can you please help clarify this?" If you are the coach, sit in silence for a minute, and then ask your client the following. If you are facilitating pairs, encourage them to ask questions such as the following:
   - What emotions did you just experience as you said that?
   - How did you manage those emotions just now, and how can you manage them during the actual conversation with your boss?

9. Brainstorm ways to manage other difficult emotions so that the conversation with the boss can stay focused on the content. Ask questions such as:
   - What fears come up for you as you anticipate your boss's response to this conversation? What hopes?
   - What is the worst-case scenario? How likely is it? What can you tell yourself that will help you prepare for it if it happens? What is the best-case scenario? How likely is it? What can you say to yourself that will help you evoke this response?

- When are other times you have had difficult conversations and had a successful outcome? What did you do to influence that response? What emotions did you experience and utilize that influenced your success, or lack of success, in that difficult conversation?

10. Encourage them to schedule this meeting with the boss, and then if you are coaching an individual have a follow-up conversation with the client to support his or her efforts, to celebrate successes during and as a result of the conversation, and to explore areas in which he or she experienced intense emotions that invite additional skill-building. If this is a group exercise, set a follow-up session for this conversation.

Tip

Caution your clients not to blame the boss or spend too much time talking about what has gone wrong in the past. Instead, make the focus of the conversation about how behavior will be different in the future to enhance the employee-boss relationship. This approach will inevitably lead to a stronger and more positive series of interactions between the client and boss. By helping them to take responsibility for initiating this vital conversation, they often feel empowered to manage the relationship more openly in the future.

THE ESSENTIAL CONVERSATION HANDOUT

Instructions: Using a 1 to 5 scale, rate the following relationship characteristics with your current boss. Put the appropriate number in the blank after each item.

1 = Poor   2 = Fair   3 = Average   4 = Good   5 = Excellent

1. We communicate frequently. _____

2. We communicate about the right things. _____

3. We have a positive relationship. _____

4. My boss recognizes me for my efforts. _____

5. We understand each other. _____

6. My boss utilizes my strengths. _____

7. My boss gives me opportunities to grow and develop. _____

8. My boss and I deal with conflict effectively. _____

CHAPTER 5

Decision Making*

"The application of emotion to manage change and solve problems."

This EISA factor measures your ability to:

- Use positive emotions
- Use negative emotions
- Manage change and emotions to solve problems

Emotions are a factor in every decision, whether conscious or not. Some people claim, "I never let emotions get in the way of my decisions. I follow the same rational, logical process for every decision I make, and I do all I can to be unemotional about the problem and the solution." However, it is not recommended or even possible to separate emotions from the decision-making process. In fact, emotions—if accurately incorporated—will enhance the appropriateness and effectiveness of any decision.

---

*The introductory material in this section is derived from S. Stein, D. Mann, P. Papadogiannis, and W. Gordon (2010), *The Emotional Intelligence Skills Assessment (EISA) Facilitators' Guide*. San Francisco, CA: Pfeiffer.

Positive emotions can provide more confidence in any decision. How many risky business decisions have turned into extraordinary success due to optimism and confidence? But what if so much optimism is allowed that important serious considerations are overlooked? How many decisions have been rushed—such as the purchasing of a new home or the hiring of a new employee—because of strong positive feelings and a disregard for other important guiding information?

A facile use of differing emotions to fit a situation supports effective decision making. It may be tempting to try to avoid difficult emotions, such as stress and anxiety. Yet some amount of stress or concern actually heightens awareness and allows one to process more detailed information. Additionally, a quiet mood provides the opportunity for all involved to reflect on important considerations before reaching a decision.

Who wants his or her tax attorney in a festive mood while she is defending his or her case? Who would feel at his or her creative best in a brainstorming session if he or she were forced to hear about the latest dire corporate news? Someone skilled at decision making recognizes what emotions will best enhance a particular situation and is able to match the situation with his or her emotions to manage change or to develop the best solution to a problem.

People skilled in decision making can adjust their moods to the task at hand; they can be subdued when attending to details and more elevated when the situation is appropriate for engaging others' optimism and humor. Their gut-reaction decisions are sound, demonstrating their ability to effectively match their moods with situations.

Mood can play an enormous role in the accuracy of decisions. Effective decision making is the ability to build on emotions—including those emotions acknowledged in developing strong perceiving and managing skills—and to incorporate additional environmental information to deal with change or develop appropriate solutions. The following three exercises are for building the skill of decision making.

EXERCISE 5.1. EMOTIONS INFORM DECISIONS

Purpose

To help clients develop awareness of the crucial role emotions play in the decision-making process.

Thumbnail

30 minutes

Clients identify a current situation in which an important decision needs to be made; brainstorm possible solutions; and explore emotions connected with each potential option. They then practice a reflective, intuitive process that helps them further generate and incorporate new emotional information into their decision making.

Outcomes

Clients will recognize that emotions always affect decision making and will become more skillful in utilizing the data and guidance those emotions provide to enhance effective decision making.

Audience

- Individuals in coaching session or group training
- Intact teams
- Individual team members desiring to build skills to take back to the team
- Team leaders

Facilitator Competencies

 Moderate

Materials

- Pens
- Emotions Inform Decisions Handout

Time Matrix

Exercise	Estimated Time
Discuss how emotions affect decisions	5 minutes
Fill out Emotions Inform Decisions Handout	20 minutes
Discuss	5 minutes
Total Time	**30 minutes**

Instructions

1. Introduce this exercise by explaining the fallacy of the belief that decisions can be made without factoring in emotional data. In truth, all information that comes to our awareness is first processed through the emotional part of the brain, the limbic system, before our brain engages in rational processing. Successful decision making, therefore, requires accurate awareness of emotions and effective use of this emotional information. Discuss how crucial it is that one be aware of the role emotions play in the decision-making process. Ask for examples of what has happened to your coachee or the group/team you're working with when they failed to acknowledge or regulate emotions in themselves or others. Also guide them to increase their awareness of what happened when their engagement with someone in a joint decision-making situation evoked resistant or angry responses. Was the outcome just bad, or even catastrophic, as a result?

2. Distribute the Emotions Inform Decisions Handout and ask everyone to:
   - Fully think through a situation in which they need to make an important decision.
   - Briefly describe the situation, let themselves engage in creative brainstorming about possible solutions, and then write down several potential decisions. Some options are likely to feel like excellent ones, while others may seem even a bit silly.
   - Write at least three emotions that come up immediately when they think of each option.

Developing Emotional and Social Intelligence

3. Now tell them to choose two or a maximum of three solutions that seem plausible and, for each of these options, imagine it is some time in the future and that decision was made. Say: "Check out how it feels, notice what you see, what you and others are saying about the decision. Then just give yourself a quiet moment to be with that decision. Breathe and relax. What does your intuition tell you about the decision?"

4. Once they have finished this process with their first potential solution, instruct them to calmly proceed to giving the same consideration to their other one or two solutions.

5. After they have completed this process with their two or three selected options, ask them to reflect on what they have gained from all this new information. Encourage them to use this information intentionally as they make this decision. If they are not already clear on the best way to go, suggest they discuss (if possible) all this feedback with a trusted person or group that will be affected by the decision. If you are presenting this to a team, guide team members to discuss the possibilities together.

6. Lead a discussion about what was learned and how to work with their decisions. Ask them how they can extrapolate the learning from this process to other important decisions.

Tip

Discuss the consideration that awareness of emotions enhances clients' effective use of both intuitive decision making as well as fact-based decision-making skills.

EMOTIONS INFORM DECISIONS HANDOUT

Instructions: Fully think through a situation in which you need to make an important decision. Briefly describe the situation here:

1. Let yourself engage in creative brainstorming about possible solutions. Write several potential decisions below. Some are likely to feel like excellent options, while others may seem even a bit silly. For each option, write three emotions that come up immediately when you think of that option:

2. Choose two or three of the solutions you generated above that seem plausible. For each of these selected options, imagine it is some time in the future and that decision has been made. Make some notes about how it feels, notice what you see, and what you and others are saying about the decision:

3. Now give yourself a quiet moment to be with that decision. Breathe and relax. What does your intuition tell you about the decision?

Developing Emotional and Social Intelligence

4. Calmly proceed to giving the same consideration to your one or two other potential solution(s).

5. Reflect on the awareness you have gained from all this information and write your thoughts here:

EXERCISE 5.2. WHO'S IN CONTROL—YOU OR YOUR IMPULSES? DEVELOPING SELF-MASTERY

Purpose

To increase awareness of positive and negative impulses in order to understand their impact on decision making and to promote the ability to act with greater clarity and personal power.

Thumbnail

30 to 40 minutes

Clients learn about the importance of impulse control, identify several positive and negative impulses they exhibit in their lives, explore the triggers and consequences for those impulses, and develop ways to leverage positive impulses and curtail negative impulses.

Outcomes

Clients will gain insight into the emotions that drive their impulses and inform their decisions. They will then develop skills to channel those impulses in ways that are most effective for them and the people with whom they interact.

Audience

- Individuals in coaching session or group training
- Intact teams
- Individual team members desiring to build skills to take back to the team
- Team leaders

Facilitator Competencies

 Easy to Moderate

Materials

- Pens
- Who's in Control—You or Your Impulses? Developing Self-Mastery Handout

Time Matrix

Exercice	Estimated Time
Discuss the meaning and impact of impulse control	5 minutes
Write positive and negative impulses	5 minutes
Complete handout	15 to 20 minutes
Debrief	5 to 10 minutes
Total Time	**30 to 40 minutes**

Instructions

1. Discuss impulse control and the role it has in one's life. Ask your clients how they might define impulse control, and elaborate where needed. Your explanation may derive from the following description:

   Impulses are generally spontaneous, hasty, or instinctive behaviors or thoughts. The lack of impulse control gets people in all sorts of trouble. Generally speaking, the more problems people have controlling their impulses, the more difficult and complicated their lives become. Impulses can be positive, such as the desire to reach out with kindness; impulses also can make people greedy, insensitive, and thoughtless. Impulse is driven by emotion; thus it is critical to be aware of your emotions and intentional about how you use them. Some think "being emotional" is bad. That's silly, as it discounts all that drives you to be motivated to do the right thing, to care, and to be gracious. However, unregulated emotions can drive you to impulsive responses that hurt you or others. A lack of impulse control can lead you to saying things you regret or to making a decision that favors a short-term advantage despite long-term losses. Every action you take based on impulse is a choice that will have consequences for you. Some will be positive, some negative. Ineffective use of impulse control means you are not taking time to effectively choose the consequences you cause. The purpose of this exercise is to promote your increased awareness of those impulses so that you can understand their impact on your decisions and you can act with greater clarity and personal power.

2. Distribute the Who's in Control—You or Your Impulses? Developing Self-Mastery Handout and ask participants to write a list of five positive impulses they frequently exhibit. Then ask them to write a list of five challenging impulses (for ease of reference we will call those negative impulses) they frequently exhibit. Be sure to have them write the positive first or they may never recognize the positive impulses. If they have trouble thinking of positive impulses, guide them with questions such as:

   - What do you do for yourself that brings a smile to your face?
   - What do you do for others that brings a smile to their face?
   - When people compliment you, what do they mention/praise?

3. Having encouraged them to think about what works, you can then guide them to notice what impulse or driver leads them to that behavior. Samples of positive and negative impulses follow. Use these if people become stuck; however, first give them time to write their own lists. Otherwise, the power of suggestion from reading the list can unduly influence what they write.

   - *Sample positive impulses*: Love, compassion, exercising, eating healthy, taking time to get enough rest, and being successful at work.
   - *Sample negative impulses*: Judging others, over-eating, over-doing alcohol or other addictive substances, eating too much sugar, pushing oneself too hard, racing from one task to the next without taking time to breathe.

4. Ask them to reflect on their lists and choose one from each that they would like to address. Then proceed to work with the steps in the handout. Give them fifteen to twenty minutes to reflect and write. It is important that this not be rushed. Impulsive actions are habits and it takes work to change habits. If they struggle in filling out the positive skill item, here is one example: If the positive skill is eating healthy, their plan can include:

   - Giving themselves credit for this skill
   - Expanding this skill
   - Sharing the gift by giving tips of what works to others who are interested

   If they struggle with a negative impulse item, here is an example: If the negative skill is eating poorly, their plan can include:

Developing Emotional and Social Intelligence

- Taking a nutrition class
- Making a personal commitment to eating one well-balanced meal a day and then adding more balanced meals a day as they are able
- Giving up unhealthy snacks and bringing healthy snacks, such as carrots, to work

5. Bring all participants together and discuss learnings. Emphasize that changing habits takes commitment and discuss how making that commitment is worthwhile to them.

Tip

Having a supportive buddy is quite helpful when someone is working on behavior change. If you have a group of participants who can continue to be in contact, ask them to form pairs and create plans to be supportive of one another. This could be a weekly call or email, for example. Additionally, if you have the opportunity to coach over a long term, it will be useful to guide your clients to tackle another negative impulse once they have made good progress on the first one. Help them not go too fast, as the attempt to move too fast creates overwhelm rather than progress. You might want to suggest they create an affirmation or identify a behavioral trigger that reminds them of the desired change.

WHO'S IN CONTROL—YOU OR YOUR IMPULSES? DEVELOPING SELF-MASTERY HANDOUT

Instructions: Write a list of five positive impulses you frequently exhibit.

1.

2.

3.

4.

5.

Write a list of five negative impulses you frequently exhibit.

1.

2.

3.

4.

5.

Choose one from each list and answer the following questions.
Positive impulse I am exploring: _____

What triggers this impulsive response?

Are the results of my impulsive response always positive?

How does this impulsive response affect any decisions I make?

Three steps I can take to use this inclination more successfully are

1.

2.

3.

Now select one of those three and set specific intentions to act. Identify when you will take the step, what you will do, and how you will know you are successful. List how often you will apply this step before you come back to review your list and choose another step. Don't move too fast. If you truly augment this skill so it serves you and others it's worth the time! It takes commitment, paying attention, and practice to build new habits.

Negative impulse I am exploring: _____

What triggers this impulsive response?

Are the results of my impulsive response always negative?

How does this impulsive response affect any decisions I make?

Three steps I can take to change this negative impulsive response are:

1.

2.

3.

Now select one of those three and set specific intentions to act. Identify when you will take the step, what you will do, and how you will know you are successful. List how often you will apply this step before you come back to review your list and choose another step. Don't move too fast. If you truly curtail this negative impulse in a way that serves you and others, it's worth taking the time needed to gain sustainable success! It takes commitment, paying attention and practice to build new habits.

EXERCISE 5.3. DECISION MAKING, EMOTIONS, AND THINKING STYLES

Purpose

To recognize that emotions are triggered when making decisions with people who have different thinking styles and preferences.

Thumbnail

40 to 45 minutes

This exercise builds upon the theory of Emergenetics®. Participants receive information about different thinking styles and identify one they believe reflects their style. They then pair up with someone who has a different style and build their awareness of emotions and strategies that support blending the differences for success.

Outcomes

Participants recognize that there are different ways of making decisions and that working effectively with others requires an ability to understand their own emotional response to those differences. Participants also will improve their skills in working with a variety of their own and others' emotions and thinking styles.

Audience

- Individuals in group training
- Intact teams
- Team leaders

Facilitator Competencies

 Moderate

Materials

- Flip chart paper, easel, and markers (optional)
- Paper or cards to post on walls with one of the following four words written on the cards: analytical, structural, social, conceptual
- Decision Making, Emotions, and Thinking Styles Handout

Time Matrix

Exercise	Estimated Time
Pre-work—post four words on walls	5 minutes
Discuss thinking styles and emotional connection	10 minutes
Ask participants to go to the word on the wall that describes their thinking preference and invite discussion	5 to 10 minutes
Form pairs	5 minutes
Conduct role play on handout	10 minutes
Debrief results	10 minutes
Total Time	**45 to 50 minutes (not including pre-work)**

Instructions

1. Before this exercise starts, write the words analytical, structural, social, and conceptual on four separate pieces of paper. Post the words in four different parts of your training room with analytical and structural on one side and social and conceptual on the other side.

2. Explain that brain research has found that humans have different preferences for thinking about an issue and thus different styles in making decisions. Those differences trigger emotional responses. For example, someone with a preference to be very analytical, to think things through carefully and research well, may feel frustrated when he or she is making a decision with a person who has primarily a social thinking style. The person with a social preference will care what the decision will mean to the people involved, but is not likely to be as interested in the analysis. A good decision incorporates both types of considerations, but emotional resistance to the differences can prevent or limit people's ability to work together.

   This exercise will draw on the system of understanding differences presented through Emergenetics®. You can learn more at www .emergenetics.com and www.cgrowth.com/emergenetics.html. Most people have heard of the differences between left- and right-brain thinking. Emergenetics identifies four thinking styles and associates them with colors for ease in remembering. There are two thinking styles associated with left-brain thinking—analytical (blue) and structural (green)—and two thinking styles associated with right-brain thinking—social (red) and conceptual (yellow).

Your participants will understand the core concepts with the following key attributes, derived from Emergenetics (Browning, 2006). This information is contained in the handout so your participants can reference it easily.

Analytical
Results-oriented
Fact-based foundation
Strategic thinker
Leads by taking responsibility

Learns by mental analysis

Conceptual
Fresh outlook
Intuitive about ideas
Idea person
Leads by moving the organization forward
Learns by experimenting

Structural
Practical thinker
Follow-through
Dependable
Leads by setting procedures

Learns by doing

Social
Intuitive about people
Makes contact with friends
People-oriented
Leads by networking, team building
Learns from others

3. Ask your participants to stand near the sign with the thinking style with which they feel most comfortable or to which they are most drawn. Note that most people have more than one preference, but for now they are to choose only one area. If they are comfortable in several areas, they should choose the group with the fewest people to balance the numbers in the groups. Invite discussion on why they were drawn to their particular area. Ask for specific examples of how they use this skill in making decisions. Begin with people in the analytical section, move to structural, then social, and finally to conceptual.

4. Now ask everyone on the conceptual/social side of the room to find a partner on the analytical/structural side of the room. If you have more on one side of the room, then seek to have people from the two different components on the same side (for example, analytical/structural or conceptual/social) pair up. If the extra people are in the same area, such as analytical, then ask those who feel they have a second strength in decision making to name their other preference and work to pair up with as many differences as they can. Instruct the pairs to work with the role play in the Decision Making, Emotions, and Thinking Styles Handout. Each of them should take a separate role. Point out that this is an opportunity to learn more about the differences among people and to recognize the emotions that come up for them when they are working with someone who thinks differently.

5. One person is Person A, the other is Person B. They do know each other's thinking preferences. The key point of the exercise is to use the awareness of the other person's thinking preferences to engage the partner in making a decision that the advocate believes is best.

6. Bring everyone together again to report back to the group regarding:
   - How they felt and how they used their emotional information about themselves.
   - What they noticed about the emotions of the other person as they moved through the exercise and how they worked with that information to move to success.
   - What decision they reached.

7. Ask the participants how they can have a more productive emotional engagement when working with people who approach a problem differently if they can understand the different thinking process the other person uses.

8. You can capture key points on a flip chart to promote the discussion if that fits the training situation.

Tip

The process of understanding and working with each other's preferred thinking styles and their emotional cues is the key learning. Keep most of the discussion focused on this process and awareness; the result of the role play is less important.

DECISION MAKING, EMOTIONS, AND THINKING STYLES HANDOUT

Instructions: This exercise is built on working with four thinking styles as defined by Emergenetics (Browning, 2006). Read the descriptions below and select an area or areas that reflect how you believe you make decisions.

Definition of Attributes

Analytical
Results-oriented
Fact-based foundation
Strategic thinker
Leads by taking responsibility

Learns by mental analysis

Structural
Practical thinker
Follow-through
Dependable
Leads by setting procedures

Learns by doing

Conceptual
Fresh outlook
Intuitive about ideas
Idea person
Leads by moving the
organization forward
Learns by experimenting

Social
Intuitive about people
Makes contact with friends
People-oriented
Leads by networking, team
building
Learns from others

Role Play Instructions for Person A: The Advocate

You want to get an exciting new project launched, done well, and completed on time, which, given how exciting this project is, should be soon. It's a challenging project and would take others a few months, but you believe this is so valuable that other projects should be put to the side and this should be finished in one month. [Feel free to work with Person B and make up the nature of the project so that it's something that fits the type of work you do. If you can't think of anything, then make the project the creation of new space-age dolls in time to sell for the holidays.]

You feel:

- Excited and hopeful that this can make a difference for you and for others who will work on this project.

- Worried that you won't be able to persuade others to join in the project, especially with the same zest that you feel, so the final results won't have the potential cutting-edge results that could occur.

Your task:

- Persuade Person B to join in the project with enthusiasm.
- Use your thinking style as you decide how to present your information. Then use your best skills to actually make your case in the way that the person with the other thinking style prefers. Notice the emotions that come up for you and Person B as you negotiate.

Role Play Instructions for Person B: The One to Be Persuaded

Person A wants you to change your priorities and join in his/her project. You are reluctant to start something new and not finish what is already on your agenda. [Feel free to work with Person A and make up the nature of the project so that it's something that fits the type of work you do. If you can't think of anything, then make the project the creation of new space-age dolls in time to sell for the holidays.]

You feel:

- That "I don't think so" is the best answer, hesitant, and somewhat annoyed at the distraction from completing your other projects.
- Worried that you will have to join in the project and that you will lose traction on other important projects that could have good results for you.

Your task:

- Decide whether to join in the project. Don't be too quick to say yes or too insistent on saying no. Take time to practice these skills and ulti- mately be cooperative.
- Use your thinking style as you decide how to present your responses. Then use your best skills to actually make your case in the way that the person with the other thinking style prefers. See whether you can

persuade Person A to change the project or parts of it to better meet your preferences and needs. Notice the emotions that come up for you and Person A as you negotiate.

■ ■ ■

Debrief in your pairs (once you are instructed to do so).
Talk about and take notes to report back to the group on:

- How you felt and how you used your emotional information about yourself.
- What you noticed about the emotions of the other person as you moved through the exercise and how you worked with that information to move to success.

Reference

Browning, G. (2006). *Emergenetics: Tap into the new science of success.* New York: Harper/Collins.

CHAPTER 6

Achieving*

*"The ability to generate the necessary emotions
to self-motivate in the pursuit of realistic
and meaningful objectives."*

This EISA factor measures your ability to:

- Self-motivate
- Generate necessary emotions
- Realize the pursuit of realistic and meaningful objectives

Successful people know that positive moods such as confidence and optimism help them succeed. And whether or not they are conscious about their ability to generate these positive emotions, successful people somehow find ways to sustain a positive mood. How do they do it? They seek to find meaning in all they do. They set ambitious, yet realistic goals.

---

*The introductory material in this section is derived from S. Stein, D. Mann, P. Papadogiannis, and W. Gordon (2010), *The Emotional Intelligence Skills Assessment (EISA) Facilitators' Guide*. San Francisco, CA: Pfeiffer.

They accept responsibility for achieving those goals. They acknowledge their strengths and learn how to leverage them. They welcome prompt feedback that provides them information about the success of their efforts. They look for indications of success—no matter how small—and celebrate those successes in themselves and in others.

Once generated, these positive emotions are easier to sustain. Confidence breeds more confidence; success opens the door to more success. Emotional achievers' positive moods make it easier to remain positive. Their confidence and optimism motivate them toward higher goals. They become more hopeful, more flexible. They manage stress even better. They stay focused on their goals. They are more open to vital information that will help them assess and manage risk, identify problems, and make sound decisions that solve those problems. The more effective solutions they generate, the more satisfaction they experience, the more meaning they find in their lives, and the more motivation they have to continue setting and achieving goals.

People who are not as successful in achievement are less likely to have experienced the power that positive emotions can have in their lives. They may not acknowledge that they can develop the ability to generate those emotions. They are therefore likely to feel less optimism, less confidence in themselves, and more disappointment in their lives. Just as positive emotions sustain themselves, difficult emotions also sustain themselves. This can lead to blame, burnout, risk avoidance, feelings of failure, and difficulty with change.

It is easy, although inaccurate, to think, "Emotions are just things that happen to us—we cannot help how we feel." Emotions that enhance success can actually be chosen, generated, and sustained. The following three exercises are for building the skill of achieving.

EXERCISE 6.1. EMOTIONAL WELL-BEING

Purpose

To assist participants in setting realistic goals for high achievement that also lead to high levels of authentic success and emotional well-being.

Thumbnail

25 to 40 minutes

Participants are introduced to research linking emotional intelligence, especially self-actualization, with high levels of authentic success. They are asked to write their own definitions of success, to identify personal strengths and challenges, and to consider how these interact with their values to guide achievement. They then rewrite their definitions of success after gaining these new insights.

Outcomes

Participants will develop a greater appreciation for how their values and beliefs guide their definition of, and drive for, success. With this deeper understanding, they will establish more conscious goals for achievement that will lead them to higher levels of authentic success and emotional well-being.

Audience

- Individuals in coaching session or group training
- Intact teams
- Individual team members desiring to build skills to take back to the team
- Team leaders

Facilitator Competencies

 Moderate

Materials

- Pens
- Emotional Well-Being Handout

Time Matrix

Exercise	Estimated Time
Discuss emotional well-being	5 to 10 minutes
Work on handout	10 minutes
Discuss and write second definition	5 to 10 minutes
Discuss reflection questions	5 to 10 minutes
Total Time	**25 to 40 minutes**

Instructions

1. Discuss the importance of gaining personal, team, and organizational congruence on what achieving means and how that relates to their definition of success. Ask: "Do you need all those achievements? How much is enough?" Some people are highly driven to achieve, but in the process lose or compromise many other valuable parts of their lives. Other people skate. They just don't expect enough of themselves. Ask: "Where are you on this spectrum?"

Discuss that developing awareness of the role that achieving goals has in life is central to building work/life balance. Explain that the purpose of this inquiry is to assist each participant in choosing to live a life filled with emotional well-being.

Emotional well-being is similar to the concept of self-actualization, which can be measured with questionnaires such as the EQ-i® and the EQ-360®. Dr. Reuven Bar-On, the author of these measures, has pinpointed self-actualization as the apex of all the emotional intelligence skills. When you live in emotional well-being, you experience a high level of authentic success. Bar-On named eight emotional intelligence skills that are important to achieving emotional well-being (Bar-On, 2001). He listed them in the order of their importance:
- Happiness
- Optimism
- Self-Regard
- Independence

- Problem Solving
- Social Responsibility
- Assertiveness
- Emotional Self-Awareness

One idea you can share to demonstrate how to build emotional well-being and experience the self-actualization Dr. Bar-On discusses comes from *Life's 2% Solution* (Hughes, 2006). The book presents a strategy for finding a way to engage in a truly meaningful project or activity that doesn't demand too much time. The strategy calls for taking two percent of one's time, essentially a half-hour a day, and focusing that time on oneself. During that time, the person is to do something that is personally very valuable, something he or she longs to have time to do. Some choose writing poetry, making pottery, meditating, or taking a nature walk. Discussing this strategy gives participants a way to consider the possibility that they really can make a difference in their life satisfaction.

2. Distribute the Emotional Well-Being Handout and ask the participants to answer Questions 1 through 4.

3. Ask participants to form small groups and to discuss what they have written. Then have them return to the worksheet and write their definitions of success now that they have reflected on how their strengths, challenges, and values relate to their definition.

4. Potential reflection questions you might ask include:
   - What do you observe about how your challenges interface with your values? Are there values that are dragged down by your challenge areas? What would you like to do about this insight?
   - Are you maximizing your strengths?
   - How much of your time and attention do your weaknesses receive? Is it the right proportion?
   - What do you want to do to support your current success or to enhance it?

Tip

Encourage taking enough time to be deliberate and thoughtful. A full discussion can lead to valuable quality of life interventions.

EMOTIONAL WELL-BEING HANDOUT

Instructions: Answer the questions below.

1. What does success mean to me? My definition of success is:

2. List three or four personal strengths in the table below.
3. In the table list two challenges that are real challenges to you—something that's limiting your sense of living a successful and sustainable lifestyle.
4. List up to four top values for you here and then associate those values with any of the strengths or challenges you have listed.

Strength	Strength	Strength	Strength	Challenge	Challenge
Write in your strengths or challenges in this row.					
Put the values you associate with these strengths or challenges in this row.					

5. Now respond to this statement again. My definition of success is:

How did it change from your first definition? Why did it change?

EXERCISE 6.2. COLLABORATING

Purpose

To help participants experience and further develop the positive emotions that lead to effective collaboration.

Thumbnail

35 minutes

Participants work in pairs to collaborate on a short project. They also keep an individual list of all emotions experienced during the process and explore how those emotions impacted their ability to collaborate.

Outcomes

As clients practice their skills in listening to one another and reaching a collaborative decision, they also experience and learn how to better utilize positive emotions that lead toward more collaborative achievement.

Audience

- Individuals in coaching session or group training
- Intact teams
- Individual team members desiring to build skills to take back to the team
- Team leaders

Facilitator Competencies

 Easy to Moderate

Materials

- Flip-chart paper, easel, and markers
- Pens
- Collaborating Handout

Time Matrix

Exercise	Estimated Time
Discuss the collaborative process	5 minutes
Assign a collaborative project to pairs	5 minutes
Distribute the handout, start the 7.5 minutes for the project and follow rest of handout	10 minutes
Present projects	10 minutes (more if large group)
Discuss and summarize	5 minutes
Total Time	**35 minutes (or more for large group)**

Instructions

1. Explain that there are various levels of complexity in the ways people engage with one another to make decisions. Each level in this hierarchy can have a big impact on what is achieved. People can make individual decisions or they may accommodate, cooperate, or collaborate with others in order to achieve particular goals. Each type of decision has its place. Many decisions are simple and best made by oneself. However, for more complex decisions when the goal is to have mutual buy-in by a team or group of people, collaboration is often the preferred process. Collaboration is sometimes simply defined as working with another person or group in order to achieve something. However, there's much more to the process than that definition implies. Effective collaboration means that the parties work together to share their divergent ideas with trust and are willing and able to listen to the differences in order to craft a sustainable solution that takes advantage of the creative thinking of all parties engaged. If a process is truly collaborative, all the parties will buy into the outcome and will use their best efforts to make it successful. The net result is achieving something bigger than any one person could do on his or her own.

   This process requires significant emotional intelligence. It requires an open frame of mind, a willingness to listen to ideas that might seem inefficient or otherwise off-base, and patience. It takes longer to listen and work with others than to just blast through individually to the decision. This exercise is designed to assist you in practicing the skills of listening to one another and reaching a collaborative decision so that you begin experiencing the positive emotions of achieving a successful collaboration.

2. If you are working with a group, ask them to pair up; if you are coaching an individual, work directly with your coachee. Give each pair a flip-chart page and some varied colored markers. Additional colors of markers should be available for those who believe that's an important part of their communication. Tell them they'll have 7.5 minutes to create a design that you assign. The goal is to work together to create a collaborative result and, while doing so, each person is to individually keep a running list of the emotions he or she is feeling.

   You have a choice on the design you ask them to follow. You could create it from a current situation or you can use any of the following:
   - Design a party invitation that will be successful in getting everyone at work to attend.
   - Write a poem that is four lines long and summarizes how they (or the team) work together.
   - Make it open frame—tell them to design their own project and demonstrate a collaborative result.

3. Distribute the Collaboration Handout and guide them to follow the instructions, starting with writing down their emotions while doing the project.

4. When you call time on the project, ask them to fill in Part 2 of the handout so they reflect on how they engaged with aspects of the collaboration process, and then to go on to Part 3 and write any other thoughts they would like to record.

5. Next ask all participants to post their projects, present them to the group, and describe the collaboration process they used. Wrap up with pulling together the key concepts the group has identified on how to use their emotions to promote collaboration.

Tip

One of the best ways to learn is to have fun. Make this playful.

COLLABORATING HANDOUT

Instructions: While working with your partner, keep tabs on your emotions and write them down quickly in Part 1. Don't worry about whether the feelings are good or bad; just write them down.

1. As I'm doing this project I feel:

2. After finishing the project, write your thoughts about how the following worked for you in the process and what emotions came up.

   • Openness

   • Creativity

   • Curiosity

   • Willingness to listen

   • Patience

3. Write any other reflections you have about how to expand your collaboration skills.

EXERCISE 6.3. ALIGNING YOUR POWER

Purpose

To improve clients' ability to accurately assess the power they do and do not have in specific situations so that they can more effectively use that knowledge to generate emotions that will help them achieve their goals.

Thumbnail

25 to 35 minutes

Clients identify a challenging situation and learn how to assess and compare the levels of power they perceive they have, versus the levels of power they actually have in the situation. They explore how to shift their levels of perceived power to equal the levels of actual power in order to generate and sustain the emotions needed for effective achievement. An illustrative diagram is used to introduce the concept, and the clients use this diagram to estimate how successful they are in balancing perceived power versus actual power regarding a particular situation. They then explore the impact this has on generating emotions that enhance achievement.

Outcomes

Clients will learn to recognize that difficult emotions—frustration, resignation, resistance, blaming—regarding a situation may be due not to a lack of power, but rather to a discrepancy between the power they think they have versus the power they truly have to effect a desired outcome in the situation. As they learn to adjust their perceived power to better reflect the reality of their situations, it will enable them to generate the positive emotions that lead to and sustain achievement.

Audience

- Individual working with a coach or team leader
- Individual team members desiring to build skills to take back to the team
- Team leaders

Facilitator Competencies

 Moderate

Materials

- Pens
- Paper

Time Matrix

Exercise	Estimated Time
Clients identify and explore a challenging situation, including assessment of own power in situation	5 to 10 minutes
Introduce concept and diagram of perceived versus actual power	10 minutes
Clients explore emotional impact of situations where perceived/actual power was balanced or not, and effect on achievement	5 to 10 minutes
Summarize and plan for future skill building	5 minutes
Total Time	**25 to 35 minutes**

Instructions

1. Begin this exercise by asking your clients to identify current situations in which they would like to make changes but don't feel powerful enough to do so.
2. Then ask your clients the following questions:
   - What makes this situation so challenging for you?
   - What do you want to see happen that isn't happening right now?
   - What is preventing the desired result from happening?
   - In what ways do you wish you had more power or control to fix this situation?

   Clients generally do not have much difficulty answering these questions. However, if they are stuck, encourage them to think about times when they may have felt emotions such as anger, hopelessness, frustration, fear, or lack of control, as these emotions often accompany situations in which people feel powerless.

3. Next, ask your clients to consider areas where they do have power in the situation. This is generally a more difficult question to answer. You may hear, "I don't have any power; that's why it's so frustrating." If so, remind them that everyone has some power, at least regarding how he or she thinks about and responds to the situation. Encourage continued brainstorming by asking, "Where else do you have power?" Alternately, you may have to challenge them to more accurately assess areas in which they perceive power that is not real. One example of this is the desire (but not power) to change another person. You may need to encourage clients to expand their definitions of power if they are narrow (for example, "Only people with an official title have power") or to limit the definitions if they are global ("I can do anything I set my mind to; I just need to get others to see things my way").

4. Now explore how well your clients assessed their actual power. Rarely do clients accurately identify their levels of power. They often overlook areas where they do have power, focus where they are lacking, or become frustrated because they think they should be able to change something they cannot. Explain to them that it is often not the amount of actual power, but rather this discrepancy between perceived and actual power, that limits achievement. The more realistic people are about what power they do and do not have, the more successful they will be in generating emotions to motivate them to achieve their goals. They will create an attitude that inspires them to work for what they truly can achieve instead of becoming frustrated by striving for something that is not possible.

5. Suggest that those who are more accurate in assessing their own power also have a more positive emotional impact on others. To demonstrate, ask your clients:
   - When have you interacted with people who did not assess or use their power well, for example, people who had a lot of power but acted as if they did not have any? Or those who had very little power but acted as if they ran the world?
   - What impact did those people have on you? On others?
   - How successful were they in achieving what they wanted to achieve?

6. Now draw a diagram for your clients similar to the diagram below. Suggest that the more accurate and aware people are of the power they have, the more effective they can be at achieving their goals. Ask:
   - What is the effect when people have no power but act as if they do? (This behavior could be named arrogance.)
   - What is the effect when people have a lot of power but do not recognize it and act unconsciously as if they do not have power? (This behavior could be named ignorance.)

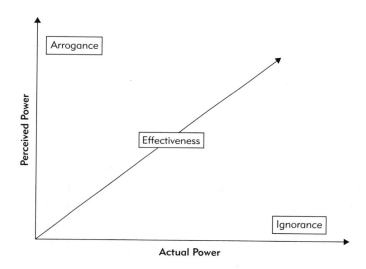

   - Where on this diagram are people more likely to be seen as controlling? As collaborative? (Some people are controlling because they don't feel they have enough power. Some people are collaborative because they feel they have enough power and can therefore share it.)
7. Ask your clients:
   - Regarding the challenging situation you identified today, where would you place yourself right now on this diagram?
   - Where were you on this diagram before our discussion?
   - If your position changed, have your emotions shifted as a result?
   - If so, how might these new emotions impact your ability to more effectively achieve your goals?
8. Finally, ask clients how to continue accurately assessing their power regarding situations in the future. Remind them that emotions are a

great ally in this effort. If they are feeling frustrated, angry, defensive, discouraged, hopeless, resigned, resisting change, or desperately wanting to control a situation, they might well need to balance perceived versus actual power. Encourage them also to identify people who assess and use their power well to achieve, as they can serve as inspiring role models:

- Who is the most powerfully effective person you know? This could be someone with a lot of power who uses it well, or it could be someone with very little power who still finds a way to be effective despite a lack of control over many situations.
- What power does this person have, and how does he or she use it well?
- What power does he or she not have, and how does he or she keep that from getting in the way?

Tip

Clients often experience great relief when they discover that they have more power than they thought they did. (For example, your client may realize that others might be resisting his or her ideas because those ideas were presented too powerfully rather than not powerfully enough.) Clients also experience relief if they recognize that they are creating unnecessary pain for themselves by trying to change something they are not able to control. This feeling of relief helps lead them toward even more powerful positive emotions that inspire the achievement they are seeking. This exercise also links well to priority-setting and decision-making activities, as it helps clients more effectively evaluate the likelihood of success with a variety of alternatives.

CHAPTER 7

Influencing*

> *"The ability to recognize, manage, and evoke emotion within oneself and others to promote change."*

This EISA factor measures your ability to:

- Appraise a situation
- Interpret emotional tone
- Evoke emotions
- Promote change

While achieving is the ability to generate positive emotions for individual motivation, influencing is the ability to introduce this process in others. The fifth and final EISA factor of influencing incorporates aspects of all the factors before it. The more skilled one becomes at emotional perceiving, managing, decision making, and achieving, the more

---

*The introductory material in this section is derived from S. Stein, D. Mann, P. Papadogiannis, and W. Gordon (2010), *The Emotional Intelligence Skills Assessment (EISA) Facilitators' Guide.* San Francisco, CA: Pfeiffer.

successful one will be in influencing. In other words, to influence someone else, self-knowledge is required. Skilled influencers need to know themselves—to accurately perceive what they are feeling, what encourages them, what drives them. They also need to know how to effectively manage those emotions and to express themselves to others in order to sustain successful interactions. They have to learn how to interpret information from others to allow for the most complete information sharing for making sound decisions. They learn to generate desired emotions in themselves to make changes and achieve goals and to inspire a similar process in others. This last step is influencing.

How often do people accept advice from others? When are suggestions from others readily implemented, even if those suggestions might make a significant positive change in a person's life? Not as often as would serve most people. This is partly because the messenger often does not have a sufficient understanding of the recipient's emotional experience.

Effective influencing also requires that the messenger have an understanding of how others perceive him or her. Those offering guidance may consider themselves to be wise, approachable, and competent, but do others view them that way? If not, the recipients of the information will be having a less positive emotional experience and therefore will be less likely to listen to or implement any ideas suggested. Perhaps they see the messenger as angry, aggressive, controlling, or impulsive, which elicits feelings of anger, fear, and defensiveness. Perhaps they think the suggestion is too logical, and that may provoke a more emotional response in an effort to provide a kind of balance in the interaction. Further, if body language and tone of voice do not match words, intentions will be misread and resisted.

On the other hand, if those receiving the suggestions feel understood, respected, and acknowledged, and think that the messenger is optimistic about their success, they are more likely to be open to the new information and inspired to set and achieve new goals as a result. If they have confidence, they will be more energized and motivated to work together toward a common goal. The following three exercises are for building this skill of influencing.

EXERCISE 7.1. BE A MAGNET

Purpose

To develop participants' awareness of their current level of influencing skills in order to improve these skills in future interactions.

Thumbnail

10 to 20 minutes, plus individual time

Participants are asked to focus daily for one week on a situation in which they are seeking to influence a person or a decision. They are also asked to spend fifteen minutes at the end of each day to write about that interaction. A handout with questions for each day is provided to structure the fifteen-minute reflection session.

Outcomes

Clients will gain awareness of their levels of effectiveness in using emotions to influence others. This awareness will help them choose more successful influencing strategies in the future.

Audience

- Individuals in coaching session or group training
- Intact teams
- Individual team members desiring to build skills to take back to the team
- Team leaders

Facilitator Competencies

 Easy

Materials

- Be a Magnet Handout

Time Matrix

Activity	Estimated Time
Explain the process of influencing	5 minutes
Assign a reflection activity for seven days and give the handout with the questions	5 minutes (plus 15 minutes a day individual reflection time)
Review what has been written and form intentions	0 minutes in group (part of the 15 minutes a day individual reflection time)
Discuss whether they come together again	0 to 10 minutes
Total Time	**10 to 20 minutes (plus individual time)**

Instructions

1. Explain that influencing is based on self-knowledge. Influencers need to know how to effectively manage their emotions and to express themselves to others in order to sustain successful interactions. They need to learn how to interpret information from others to allow for the most complete information sharing for making sound decisions. They learn to generate desired emotions in themselves to make changes, to achieve goals, and to inspire a similar process in others.

2. In order to build awareness and effectiveness in influencing others, coach your coachee or the group you are working with to heighten their awareness of how they currently influence others. Ask them to focus daily during the next week on an interaction in which they are seeking to influence a person or a decision. Also ask them to take fifteen minutes at the end of each day to write about that interaction. Provide them with the handout with the questions to answer.

3. At the end of the seven days, they should thoughtfully review what has been written and form intentions for future actions.

4. If you will be working with them again, ask them to bring in their work and discuss it. If you will not be working with them again, suggest they find an accountability partner with whom they can discuss their experiences and their long-term action plans.

Tip

Emphasize that they will get out of this exercise what they put into it. Thoughtful introspection can give them solid recognition of strategies that are supporting success in influencing as well as ones that are sabotaging their success.

BE A MAGNET HANDOUT

Instructions: Complete the following set of questions every day for seven days.

Day One
Summarize the event and your purpose:

While I was engaged in influencing the person or outcome, I felt:

After today's engagement finished, I felt:

How well did I use my emotional awareness and tie it to the purpose of the situation? Why was I successful?

What was quite successful so I want to remember to repeat it?

What could I do better next time?

Day Two

Summarize the event and your purpose:

While I was engaged in influencing the person or outcome, I felt:

After today's engagement finished, I felt:

How well did I use my emotional awareness and tie it to the purpose of the situation? Why was I successful?

What was quite successful so I want to remember to repeat it?

What could I do better next time?

Day Three
Summarize the event and your purpose:

While I was engaged in influencing the person or outcome, I felt:

After today's engagement finished, I felt:

How well did I use my emotional awareness and tie it to the purpose of the situation? Why was I successful?

What was quite successful so I want to remember to repeat it?

What could I do better next time?

Day Four
Summarize the event and your purpose:

While I was engaged in influencing the person or outcome, I felt:

After today's engagement finished, I felt:

How well did I use my emotional awareness and tie it to the purpose of the situation? Why was I successful?

What was quite successful so I want to remember to repeat it?

What could I do better next time?

Day Five
Summarize the event and your purpose:

While I was engaged in influencing the person or outcome, I felt:

After today's engagement finished, I felt:

How well did I use my emotional awareness and tie it to the purpose of the situation? Why was I successful?

What was quite successful so I want to remember to repeat it?

What could I do better next time?

Day Six

Summarize the event and your purpose:

While I was engaged in influencing the person or outcome, I felt:

After today's engagement finished, I felt:

How well did I use my emotional awareness and tie it to the purpose of the situation? Why was I successful?

What was quite successful so I want to remember to repeat it?

What could I do better next time?

Day Seven
Summarize the event and your purpose:

While I was engaged in influencing the person or outcome, I felt:

After today's engagement finished, I felt:

How well did I use my emotional awareness and tie it to the purpose of the situation? Why was I successful?

What was quite successful so I want to remember to repeat it?

What could I do better next time?

Intentions
Having reviewed this information, I intend to:

EXERCISE 7.2. ENGAGED LISTENING

Purpose

To teach clients how to use the effective power of engaged listening in order to be influential in promoting change.

Thumbnail

25 minutes

Clients work in pairs (or one-on-one with a coach) to practice engaged and influential listening following a six-step L.I.S.T.E.N. model: Listen, Inquire, Silence, Talk, Empathy, and Negotiation.

Outcomes

Clients will learn an easy-to-remember model for listening that they can incorporate into future interactions; they will experience the challenge of listening effectively with the opportunity for immediate feedback; and they will increase their success in influencing others in a positive way as they improve their engaged listening skills.

Audience

- Individuals in group training
- Intact teams
- Individual team members desiring to build skills to take back to the team
- Team leaders

Facilitator Competencies

 Easy to Moderate

Materials

- Engaged Listening Handout

Time Matrix

Activity	Estimated Time
Discuss the process of influencing and especially the key role of listening in that process	5 minutes
Distribute the handout; form pairs; and ask participants to take five minutes each listening and employing the six steps and then debrief in their pairs	15 minutes
Discuss and wrap up	5 minutes
Total Time	**25 minutes**

Instructions

1. Discuss what it means to be a good influencer. Review the four EISA factors presented in the overview:
   - Appraise a situation
   - Interpret emotional tone
   - Evoke emotions
   - Promote change

   Additionally, consider other statements of positive influence. For example, a great many people have been influenced by the Dale Carnegie approach. Ask what approaches others have used.

   A key tool to promote change is to listen well to someone else and then to add empathic questions that are respectful while evoking change. This exercise is about using the effective power of listening and engaging.

2. Guide your group to talk with one another in pairs about a situation that has a mid-level of importance to them; if you are working with an individual client, your client will be working directly with you. The person sharing the story is to fully and honestly talk and participate. The person listening is to apply the following six-step process while listening and engaging.
   - Listen
   - Inquire

- Silence
- Talk
- Empathy
- Negotiate

3. Distribute the Engaged Listening Handout and ask them to choose the first speaker. The listener engages by using the six actions in the handout. After five minutes, have them change roles so both practice being the one who influences through engaged listening.

4. Wrap up by bringing the group back together and discussing their experiences as both listener and speaker. What did the listeners do that influenced the speakers in a positive way? What emotions did all experience as they participated in this exercise?

Tip

This looks simple, yet it takes considerable work to do well. Encourage participants to create a stretch goal for themselves through using this six-step process on a frequent basis.

ENGAGED LISTENING HANDOUT

Instructions: When you are the one listening, apply the following in order to engage and influence change. Be respectful. Whether you are involved or not in the event the speaker is describing, you can influence a change by assisting the speaker in making his or her own useful decisions.

- **Listen**—Pay attention to all you are hearing as well as to the nonverbal data.
- **Inquire**—Ask respectful questions for clarity and to help focus the conversation.
- **Silence**—Be quiet, listen, and notice.
- **Talk**—Speak with engagement and respect; don't change the topic.
- **Empathy**—Actively let your colleague know you care through your personal engagement and your questions and comments.
- **Negotiate**—Ask questions that lead to helping your colleague gain better clarity; don't try to win. You are using this to reach better understanding.

EXERCISE 7.3. ACHIEVE YOUR G.O.A.L. WITH EFFECTIVE FEEDBACK

Purpose

To help clients influence other individuals toward a positive outcome by delivering feedback, especially challenging feedback, in a way that elicits positive emotions in both the person giving the feedback and in the recipient.

Thumbnail

50 minutes

Clients learn a model acronym "G.O.A.L." for delivering specific feedback that incorporates all parties' goals and motivations as part of the feedback process. This enhances the recipient's positive emotional response to the information so that he or she is more likely to be receptive to the feedback and make positive behavioral changes.

Outcomes

Clients will improve their ability to manage and evoke emotions that promote positive behavioral changes. This will also enhance clients' relationships, as they will learn to deliver positive and challenging feedback in a way that motivates others to achieve their goals, which can deepen trust and respect among parties.

Audience

- Individuals in coaching session or group training
- Intact teams
- Individual team members desiring to build skills to take back to the team
- Team leaders

Facilitator Competencies

Moderate

MATERIALS

- Pens
- Paper
- Achieve Your G.O.A.L. Handout

Time Matrix

Activity	Estimated Time
Introduce the topic of delivering effective feedback; clients review handout and identify person to whom they will give feedback	5 minutes
Clients complete handout	25 minutes
Clients explore ways to facilitate upcoming conversation and practice delivering the feedback	15 minutes
Clients schedule time with recipients	5 minutes
Debrief with clients after feedback is delivered	Varies depending on depth of follow-up discussion
Total Time	**50 minutes, plus delivery of feedback and follow-up discussion**

Instructions

1. Explain that people are more open to feedback and influence if they have a goal they want to achieve, if they feel that that goal is understood, and if they believe the feedback will help them achieve that goal. Help your clients understand that every individual is motivated by different factors; so in order to evoke emotion within another to promote positive change, the first step is to understand what motivates that person. Then explain that the purpose of this exercise is to coach the clients in how to give effective feedback to others.
2. Ask your clients to:

- Turn to the Achieve Your G.O.A.L. handout. Note that this is the model they will be using.
- Identify a situation in which they want to influence or help motivate someone to change a behavior and describe that situation in the space provided on the handout. The situation could be either a positive or a challenging situation, but has to be one in which the other person demonstrated an observable behavior.
- Consider their goals for giving feedback to this other person. For example, you can ask your clients: "What are your hopes and dreams for this person? Why are you investing in this discussion?"
- Identify the other person's potential goals and motivations. What matters to him or her? A promotion? Recognition for excellent work? More flexible hours?
- Write a brief, positive statement to say to the other person that incorporates both sets of goals and motivations. For example, one of your clients might write: "I am pleased we are on this team together. We are both invested in the outcome, and you have worked hard to generate creative options for the problems we are trying to solve."
- Briefly, objectively, and specifically describe the chosen situation, reflecting the other person's observed behavior without judgment. For example: "In our team meeting yesterday when I suggested we spend more time exploring Plan C, you stood up, rolled your eyes, and said, 'We all know Plan C isn't going to work.'"
- Identify how this person's behavior affected them. Encourage your clients to use words that appropriately describe their feelings. For example, one of your clients might decide to say to the other person: "I was disappointed that you didn't want to hear my ideas about Plan C, and I felt disrespected that you would bring it up in front of the group instead of talking to me about it one-on-one."
- Explore what positive or negative impact the other person's behavior had on your clients' long-term hopes for the relationship. For example, your clients might decide to share with the other person: "I want us to be able to continue working well together on this team. I have such respect for you and the ideas you bring to our meetings, which is what made this situation even harder for me."

3. Guide your clients to plan on how to encourage the other person to share his or her long-term hopes for the relationship or situation when this conversation takes place and to acknowledge that whatever comes out of the discussion will deepen both of their goals and motivations, therefore benefiting both. For example: "I think our different points of view will strengthen the final outcome of our project, and I want to find a respectful way for us to express those differences so we encourage, rather than discourage, each other. What are you thinking about all this?"

4. Ask your clients what possible supportive and challenging responses they might anticipate from the other person and help prepare your clients for a constructive response.

5. Have your clients practice delivering this feedback with you or in pairs if you are working with a group. Emphasize the importance of your clients being in an open and relaxed mood, making their comments brief (taking less than one minute to deliver), and being prepared to facilitate a positive discussion afterward.

6. Guide your clients to schedule a time to deliver the feedback to the appropriate person, and then schedule a time to debrief the outcome afterward if possible.

7. *Optional Stretch Goal:* Incorporate this exercise with one of the Perceiving exercises in this section of the book to help your clients accurately perceive their emotions and the emotions and motivations of the person receiving feedback.

Tip

The more this exercise is practiced, the more powerful and natural it becomes. Encourage your clients to find simple ways to incorporate it into their daily lives.

ACHIEVE YOUR G.O.A.L. WITH EFFECTIVE FEEDBACK HANDOUT

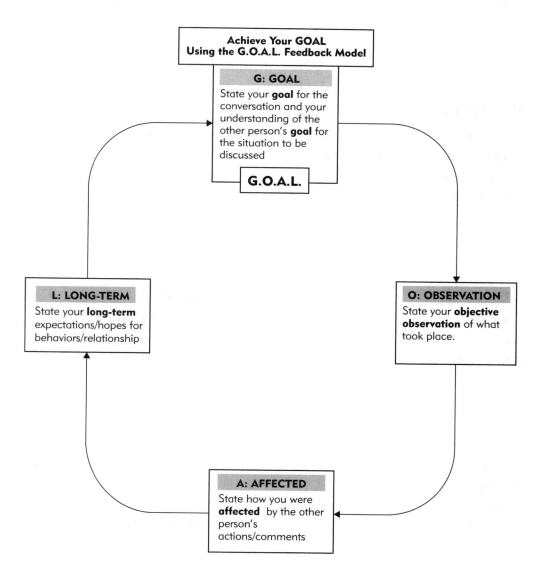

Achieve Your GOAL
Using the G.O.A.L. Feedback Model

G: GOAL
State your **goal** for the conversation and your understanding of the other person's **goal** for the situation to be discussed

G.O.A.L.

O: OBSERVATION
State your **objective observation** of what took place.

A: AFFECTED
State how you were **affected** by the other person's actions/comments

L: LONG-TERM
State your **long-term** expectations/hopes for behaviors/relationship

continued

I. The Situation

This is the situation in which I want to motivate someone to change his or her perceptions or behavior. (*Example*: "I want my co-worker to be more supportive in team meetings when we are brainstorming possible solutions.")

II. Mutual Goals

This is my goal (positive intent) for this situation and relationship. (*Example*: "My co-worker is smart, creative, and can be supportive of my ideas at times. I can see that we will be working together for a long time, which could be good for both of us.")

This is what I understand this person's goal(s) and motivations to be. (*Example*: "I think this co-worker likes to be recognized for his creativity. He likes to solve problems. He also cares about what I think of him and wants me to respect his ideas.")

Here is a positive statement I can say to this person that incorporates joint goals and motivations. (*Example*: "I am pleased we are on this team together. We are both invested in the outcome, and you have worked hard to generate creative options for the problems we are trying to solve.")

III. Objective Observations

Here is how I can share my observations of this person's behavior. Be specific and objective, no judgment or generalities. (*Example*: "In our team meeting yesterday when I suggested we spend more time exploring Plan C, you stood up, rolled your eyes, and said, 'We all know Plan C isn't going to work.'")

IV. How I Was Affected

Here is how I can share some of the ways I was affected by his or her behavior. (Describe your emotions. *Example*: "I was disappointed that you didn't want to hear my ideas about Plan C, and I felt disrespected that you would bring it up in front of the group instead of talking to me about it one-on-one.")

V. Long-Term

Here are some of the positive or negative impacts this person's behavior had on my long-term hopes for our relationship. (*Example*: "I want us to be able to continue working well together on this team. I have such respect for you and the ideas you bring to our meetings, which is what made this situation even harder for me.")

VI. Goals

This statement will reflect my understanding of the overall goals both of us have for our working or personal relationship and my hope that we can have a conversation that will enhance them. (Use a statement to tie your feedback to your first goal statement and to encourage discussion for future improvement. *Example:* "I think our different points of view will strengthen the final outcome of our project, and I want to find a respectful way for us to express those differences so we encourage, rather than discourage, each other. What are you thinking about all this?")

PART THREE

Exercises to Build
Emotionally Intelligent
Teams, Organized in
the Seven Categories
of the TESI®

Competency	*Time to Complete Exercise*
Team Identity	
8.1 Team Identity Scavenger Hunt	25 minutes
8.2 Walk in My Shoes	35 minutes
8.3 Building Team Values	10 minutes
Team Motivation	
9.1 Success Through Being on Target	35 to 45 minutes
9.2 Attitude Rules Motivation	45 to 60 minutes
9.3 Focusing on Inspiration	15 to 20 minutes
Team Emotional Awareness	
10.1 Name That Emotion	30 minutes
10.2 Noticing Emotions	30 minutes
10.3 Paying Attention to Us	35 to 45 minutes
Team Communication	
11.1 Listening with the Ears of Your Heart	50 minutes
11.2 Diversity Mania	25 minutes
11.3 Turn Off Email!	30–35 minutes
Team Stress Tolerance	
12.1 Work and Play	65 minutes
12.2 When the Internet Is Down	35 to 50 minutes
12.3 Energizers and Stress Triggers	40 to 55 minutes
Team Conflict Resolution	
13.1 SWOT Your Team Conflict	65 to 70 minutes
13.2 Judging or Open-Minded?	50 minutes
13.3 To Confront or Not to Confront	50 minutes
Team Positive Mood	
14.1 Cultural Fest	2 hours
14.2 Recognition Cubes	20 minutes
14.3 Rounds of Appreciation	40 to 60 minutes

CHAPTER 8

Team Identity

*"How well the team demonstrates belongingness,
a desire to work together, and a sense of clarity
around the role of each member."**

Team Identity is the first of the seven core skills for team emotional and social intelligence. There are two key aspects of team identity. First, team members must find something about the team that is similar to something about each individual team member. For example, all team members are leaders, IT professionals, or line staff from various areas of the organization; all members are marketing managers; or all members are people who have volunteered for a committee. The goal is for every member to create a personal association and sense of unity with the team so that each person wants to be known as a member of that team. When team members have identified with the team, the team becomes a problem-solving organism that is larger than the sum of its parts.

---

*M. Hughes & J.B. Terrell. (2009). *Team Emotional and Social Intelligence Facilitator's Guide–TESI® Short*. San Francisco: Pfeiffer.

The second part of team identity is composed of the view of the team as a whole. It is the team's reputation as a distinct unit with its own personality and credibility. This largely is an external view, reflecting how others who work with your team perceive or view the team. For example, your team might be perceived as a fun team, a serious team, or an effective team. You will also have a view of your team, which may be similar to or different from others' perspectives.

When team identity is developed at a high level, team members will have strong allegiance, demonstrated by a self-renewing collaborative effort by individuals who feel they belong and are appreciated for their contributions.

A mixture of components builds identity within a team. Key attributes are

1. Sense of purpose
2. Acceptance of one another
3. Perception that the team is a distinct entity
4. Commitment to the team and its purpose
5. Pride in the team
6. Clarity of roles and responsibilities
7. Resilience, including the recognition of the reality that things change

When a team has clarified its sense of purpose, it should be easy for members to understand why they are on that team and to identify with their teammates. Without this sense of purpose, they may just be attending meetings. Every aspect of clarity builds connection and potentially strengthens the team. The following three exercises will help build team identity.

EXERCISE 8.1. TEAM IDENTITY SCAVENGER HUNT

Purpose

To promote the team's awareness of the view others have of them as a team and give members an active opportunity for team engagement and reflection.

Thumbnail

25 minutes for first discussion; separate interviews 15 minutes per interview; 60 minutes or more for second discussion; 30 to 45 minutes for write-up

Introduce the topic of team identity as held externally by learning how others throughout the organization view this team. Discuss whose views and opinions are important to the team. Then divide into small groups and interview those people, and perhaps interview more individuals as awareness increases. Bring the results back to the next team meeting and discuss. Compare the team's initial self-rating to the data gathered, and develop an action plan to implement goals that result from the exercise.

Outcomes

The team will gain valuable information about how others view the team, develop a plan for managing and improving others' perception of the team, and form a stronger team identity in the process.

Audience

- Intact teams

Facilitator Competencies

 Moderate to Advanced

Materials

- Flip-chart paper, easel, and markers
- Pens
- Paper
- Team Identity Scavenger Hunt Handout

Time Matrix

Activity	Estimated Time
Introduce the topic of team identity and invite discussion	15 minutes
Divide the team into small groups and clarify assignments	10 minutes
Team members meet with interviewees	Separate meetings not during team time, with approximately 15 minutes per interview
Report back results	15 minutes per small group
Discuss and create action plan	30 minutes
Write up action plan and distribute to the team	30 to 45 minutes
Total Time	**25 minutes first discussion; 15 minutes per separate interview; 60 minutes or more, depending on number of small groups for discussion; 30 to 45 minutes for write-up**

Instructions

1. Introduce the topic of team identity, recognizing that the external view of the team is an important identity to proactively manage. Invite discussion about the people or sectors wherein the team identity is important and list those named. Ask what team members think the attitudes currently are. Next, ask team members to rate these perspectives on the following scale of 0 to 10 to gain a sense of how effective the team believes they are perceived.

Not Aware of Team	Moderately Effective	Quite Effective
0	5	10

2. Now is the time for the reality check, when the team members find out whether they are perceived as they imagine. Divide the team into

Developing Emotional and Social Intelligence

small groups of two to four people, depending on the size of the team. Assign each small group a few of the identified individuals or groups; ideally each small group would have at least three contacts. Instruct the small groups to take a week before the team gathers again and to seek specific information on the opinions of the identified individuals or groups. They can identify more individuals to interview if they find that key people were not included on the original list. (However, they should check with other groups before pursuing extra interviews so that individuals are not interviewed more than once.) When team members interview a contact, they are to fill in information on the Team Identity Scavenger Hunt Handout.

3. Talk with team members about the etiquette of the interview. Interviewees should be treated with respect, with the interviewing team members listening to the comments, even if they don't agree. They certainly can engage in a conversation by asking questions to assist in increased understanding. The team can tell the interviewee that they will be glad to get back to him or her with more information on how the team will respond if that is relevant to the discussion. However, remind them to take this statement as a commitment and to be sure to follow through.

4. Gather together in a few days and ask the small groups to report their results. Record the ratings and compare to determine how close the team's initial ratings approximated what they discovered through the interview process. Also include remarks that might increase understanding. Facilitate a discussion about opportunities to leverage strengths and address areas of potential weakness. Develop specific action goals with details on when they are to be accomplished and who will take the action.

5. Write up the action plan and distribute to team members. *Note:* You can write the action plan or have a team member do so.

6. *Optional Stretch Goal:* Check in periodically on the success of the action plan. Have teams visit those who requested a follow-up and report back to them.

Tip

Carefully discuss the interview protocol and prepare for behaviors and emotions that might be evoked. Perhaps add in a role-play interview if the team isn't familiar with doing interviews and might be defensive or avoid good data by rushing through the process. Discuss what to do if someone asks for confidentiality; the team wants to provide enough confidentiality to encourage candid feedback, yet also needs some sense of who provided the information in order to respond effectively. This exercise has the additional benefit of building personal identity with the team as well as the external identity. As teammates are hearing what others think about them and talking about that with one another, there's great opportunity to build loyalty and pride in the team. Both of these are strong components of team identity.

TEAM IDENTITY SCAVENGER HUNT HANDOUT

Instructions: Fill out this information separately for each of your contacts. Encourage your interviewee to be candid. Tell him or her that the team wants to grow and develop its success and relationships. After the interview, thank the interviewee for his or her time and candor.

Interviewee Name _____

Title or Sector _____

(*Note*: Sector might be a division within your organization, a client group, or others related to your team)

- How does he or she know our team and how well?

- How long has he or she known our team?

- How does he or she rate the team? Circle one:

  Doesn't Really Know the Team   Moderately Effective   Very Effective

What are his or her perspectives of our team?

- Strengths:

- Weaknesses:

- Opportunities:

- What else might help the team develop?

Developing Emotional and Social Intelligence

EXERCISE 8.2. WALK IN MY SHOES

Purpose

To assist team members in better understanding one another's roles and responsibilities.

Thumbnail

70 minutes for first discussion; 2 hours to exchange positions; 20 minutes follow-up discussion.

The team discusses roles and responsibilities and the relationship to building team identity. Then team members meet in pairs and prepare to exchange roles for two hours. The exchange happens during the following week. The full team meets again to discuss what they learned and the impacts to their sense of team identity.

Outcomes

The team members develop a better understanding of one another's roles and responsibilities. From this change in perspective, their ability to express empathy and cooperation expands.

Audience

- Intact teams

Facilitator Competencies

 Moderate

Materials

- None needed

Time Matrix

Activity	Estimated Time
Discuss team identity and the importance of understanding roles and responsibilities within the team	10 minutes
Form pairs and have them discuss their respective roles and responsibilities	15 minutes
As a whole team, discuss what they learned	10 minutes
During the week, team members exchange positions for at least two hours; the exchange can occur at different times	2 hours
At the next team meeting, discuss what was learned and how the team identity is affected	20 minutes
Total Time	**Approximately 3 hours**

Instructions

1. Discuss the concept of team identity and the importance that understanding each other's roles and responsibilities plays in developing a comprehensive team identity. Ask whether it's possible that some will misunderstand others' roles or responsibilities.

2. Have team members form pairs. They can choose or you can assign the pairs if you know the team well. Have them discuss their roles and responsibilities and any other key information to allow the other person to step into their shoes for two hours. The amount of time can be increased beyond two hours if appropriate, but should not be less. Set a specific time within the next week when each will fill in for the other. They don't have to trade roles at the same time.

3. Pull the full team back together for a discussion of what they have already learned and what their thoughts are about having to exchange roles. Ask how it feels to better understand one another's roles and explore responses. Tell them that you will discuss the results and observations at a follow-up team meeting in a week.

4. During the week, the team members should exchange roles as planned. This should be managed by the two team members making the exchange.

5. Meet again in a week to discuss the results. Ask questions of the team such as:
   - What did you learn?
   - Were there any surprises?
   - How will this new understanding affect your work with one another?
   - How does this promote your ability to understand and respond to one another?
   - How will this new understanding affect your engagement and collaboration within the team?
   - How does this experience change how you identify with the team?

Tip

Guide the team members to be respectful of one another as they exchange roles and to pay attention to the right time to step into one another's shoes.

EXERCISE 8.3. BUILDING TEAM VALUES

Purpose

To fortify team identity by determining team values and behaviors.

Thumbnail

40 minutes

Team members discuss the elements of positive team behaviors. They identify their top five individual team values and then agree on group team values. Finally, they create definitions including behaviors indicative of these values.

Outcomes

Team members will feel a strong sense of identity when they agree on the values that guide day-to-day behavior and decisions. Creating consensus and meaning around these values adds to the feeling of belonging, aids decision making, and motivates team members to greater achievement.

Audience

- Intact teams

Facilitator Competencies

 Moderate

Materials

- Flip-chart paper, easel, and markers
- Pens
- Building Team Values Handout

Time Matrix

Activity	Estimated Time
Create a discussion around positive team experiences, beliefs, and behaviors	5 minutes
Ask each team member to identify his or her top five team values using the Building Team Values Handout, then choose the top three values	5 minutes
Facilitate a team discussion to choose the top five team values	30 minutes
Create definitions and indicative behaviors for each of the five values	30 minutes
Total Time	**70 minutes**

Instructions

1. Lead a discussion about a positive team experience. This could be any team the members have been on or one they witnessed through a story or a movie. Ask the team members to respond to the following questions:
   - What words describe the personality of the team?
   - How did team members treat each other?
   - How were decisions made?
   - What common values seemed to guide team behavior?
2. Discuss the principle that when team members agree to a common set of guidelines or values, behaviors and decisions can align around these values. Team identity is fortified and team members build allegiance by overtly agreeing to the values and their definitions. These values serve as fundamental guideposts when there is indecision or inevitable conflict between team members. Clarifying the behaviors behind the values generates trust and respect among members. Building commitment to the team values produces a sense of pride in the unique identity that team members feel when they are part of this team.
3. Ask each team member to individually and silently start filling in the Building Team Values Handout, beginning with circling the top five values that he or she holds for this team. Next, ask each member to

choose his or her three top team values from the list of five and write them in the space provided on the handout.

4. Ask each team member to share his or her top three team values while you keep track to find the ones with the most votes. You can do this on a flip chart or on your copy of the handout. After all team members have shared their individual choices, facilitate a discussion to develop consensus on the team's top five values. List these five on a flip chart and each person can write them on his or her handout.

5. Now guide the team to create a definition for each value. Make the definition concrete by identifying at least two behaviors to support each of the values. Be sure that these behaviors can be seen in day-to-day interactions among team members.

BUILDING TEAM VALUES HANDOUT

Instructions: Individually, circle the top five team values that are most important to you. Spaces are provided to add others.

Help Others	Collaboration	Friendships
Customer Service	Serve Society	Public Service
Influence	Creativity/Innovation	Responsive to Change
Security/Stability	Recognition	Freedom
Fun	Adventure	Trust
Inquiry	Openness	Excitement
Leading the Way	Predictability	Quality
Making a Difference	Addresses Conflict	Honesty/Integrity

Now, list the top three values from the five you circled that you hold for this team. Write them in the spaces provided.

My Top Team Values

1. _____
2. _____
3. _____

After the group discussion, list the top team values as selected by the whole team. Write them in the spaces provided.

Our Top Team Values

1. _____
2. _____
3. _____
4. _____
5. _____

Fill in the following as the team develops answers.

Definitions and Two Behaviors That Demonstrate Each Value

Value	Definition	Two Observable Behaviors
1.		
2.		
3.		
4.		
5.		

CHAPTER 9

Team Motivation

"The energy levels of and responsibility within the team, and whether competition is working for or against the team."*

Team motivation is exemplified by a team's commitment to activate its three essential resources of time, energy, and intelligence—all of its intelligences: IQ and emotional and social intelligence. Teams tap into motivation via the internal state of each member—the mixture of these states form the drive for the team to execute its plan of action.

Seven ingredients form the recipe for motivating your team. They are

1. People
2. Needs
3. Desires

---

*M. Hughes & J.B. Terrell. (2009). *Team Emotional and Social Intelligence Facilitator's Guide–TESI® Short*. San Francisco: Pfeiffer.

4. Goals
5. Accountability
6. Reinforcement
7. Persistence

All of these elements must be considered from two aspects: individual team members and team goals. The seven ingredients for motivating a team are first based in the people—the members of the team. Recognizing each member and the skills he or she brings creates the opportunity to bring the gifts each one has to contribute to life. A team that recognizes the needs and desires of team members builds the capacity and desire to act. The second aspect of motivation is based in the team's goals, which are a means of organizing, having a mutually agreed-on target, and being on the same page. If team members are operating from many different directions, they are more likely to be at cross-purposes than to make progress. For any goal that is truly important for the team, team members must keep one another accountable, reinforce success, and be doggedly persistent in movement toward success of that goal. The following three exercises will help build team motivation.

EXERCISE 9.1. SUCCESS THROUGH BEING ON TARGET

Purpose

To expand motivation within the team by understanding what motivates one another, building team resonance on which actions to engage, and strategically using those actions to stimulate the team.

Thumbnail

35 to 45 minutes

The team will be creating a pie-shaped diagram with a target in the center. Each team member will write down what motivates him or her. Through dialogue, they will then integrate this information for a common reflection of strategic actions to motivate the team.

Outcomes

Team members and the leader recognize what motivates them individually and collectively. They can then strategically tap these motivations as they move forward. This builds the ability to effectively understand and respond to one another and to become more personally aware. This exercise actively and easily engages everyone in the conversation, which should support motivation on its own.

Audience

- Intact teams
- Individual team members desiring to build skills to take back to the team
- Team leaders

Facilitator Competencies

 Moderate

Materials

- Flip-chart paper and pens

Time Matrix

Exercise	Estimated Time
Discuss what motivation means	5 to 10 minutes
Have members form small groups and draw the first two circles as each person writes individually about what motivates him/her	10 minutes
Identify common motivators and put those items in the inner circle	10 minutes
Each small group presents and the team discusses the results and identifies full-team motivators	10 to 15 minutes
Total Time	**35 to 45 minutes**

Instructions

1. Discuss what it means to be motivated and the role motivation plays for the team.
2. Organize the team into small groups of three or four. If the team is five or fewer people, have them work as one unit.
3. Give each group a full-size piece of flip-chart paper and at least one colored marker per person. Ask that one member of each group draw a circle taking up most of the page and a smaller circle in the center. Then draw enough lines from the edge of the inner circle to the edge of the outer circle to create as many segments as there are members of the group, like drawing pieces of a pie. [It can be useful to draw a sample on a flip-chart page up-front.]
4. Instruct each group member to take three minutes to write down all the ways he or she is motivated to work and engage as a part of the team in his or her section of the pie.
5. Ask members of the group to discuss their ideas with one another. The goal is to find areas of common agreement regarding what is motivating and to write those in the inner circle. Another goal is to learn from one another about what motivates them individually and collectively. This can lead to new ideas, which will be good to explore in follow-up. It also leads to new capacities to be responsive to one another.

Developing Emotional and Social Intelligence

6. Once the groups are finished, ask each group to report to the team as a whole.

7. Guide a discussion among the whole team about what motivates them and how they can incorporate more motivating elements into their work. Compile a list of the common motivators. Emphasize that team members need to respond to one another effectively as they seek that which they have in common. Use this discussion to look for new or underutilized ideas and approaches.

8. *Optional Stretch Goal:* Discuss what is de-motivating and how to emphasize what does energize the team while removing the de-motivating parts.

Tip

This is a fun exercise in which you can get people up and out of their seats. Take advantage of this as a way to move around and be energized as well as to gain valuable learning, responsiveness to one another, and productivity.

EXERCISE 9.2. ATTITUDE RULES MOTIVATION

Purpose

To expand the team's intentional practice of setting the attitude and atmosphere in team meetings.

Thumbnail

45 to 60 minutes

To discuss the power of attitude. In small groups, team members explore current attitudes and then present their thoughts to the whole group. The team then sets intentions for the attitude they will express in the future.

Outcomes

Team members will understand the power of attitudes and that attitudes are chosen. Positive attitudes are a powerful motivator.

Audience

- Intact teams
- Individual team members desiring to build skills to take back to the team
- Team leaders

Facilitator Competencies

 Moderate

Materials

- Flip-chart paper, easel, and markers
- A way to post flip charts
- Attitude Rules Motivation Handout

Developing Emotional and Social Intelligence

Time Matrix

Exercise	Estimated Time
Provide background information on how attitudes affect team performance	10 minutes
In small groups, write answers to the questions	15 minutes
Come together as a whole group and present responses	10 to 20 minutes
Discuss and set intentions for the team attitudes	10 to 15 minutes
Total Time	**45 to 60 minutes**

Instructions

1. Discuss how the choices the team makes about its attitudes set the stage for success, mediocrity, or failure. Refer to the quote on the handout from Viktor Frankl's book, *Man's Search for Meaning*, about the power of attitude. Guide the team members to have an honest and exploratory discussion about the power of their attitudes. Point out that emotions are contagious—smiles and frowns are both catching. Thus, it is important that each person take responsibility for the emotional well-being of the team. Positive attitude has a powerful impact on motivation.

2. Ask the team to form small groups of two to four people, depending on the size of the team. Give each group two pieces of flip-chart paper and a marker. Ask them to discuss the questions on the handout and to write short answers on the flip-chart pages. Tell them to post their pages on a wall when they're done, and that they will be asked to talk about what they discovered. The questions on the handout include the following:
   - What attitudes does the team as a whole choose for meetings, project work, or other engagements?
   - Do the attitudes change based on the type of work? If so, how?

3. Gather the whole team back together. Ask each subgroup to post their results on the wall before they sit down. Have each group present their results. All the members should stand by their flip-chart page(s) and, even if one primarily presents for the group, ask the others to say something about the attitude they want to help create in the future.

4. After all subgroups have presented, facilitate a full discussion by the team. Ask them to write a statement of intention regarding the attitude they intend to set for team meetings and activities. Guide them to establish specifics by answering the following questions:
   - Would different attitudes serve us in different situations? If so, what are the situations?
   - What will we do specifically to build this attitude?
   - How do our individual emotions affect our team attitude? What if one of us has a bad day or something wonderful happens? How does that spill over?
   - How will we know that we are creating and maintaining the attitude we desire?
5. Write up the intentions and send to the team within a few days after the meeting.
6. *Optional Stretch Goal:* Facilitate a follow-up discussion in three to four weeks for the team to hold themselves accountable by checking on their attitudes since they set their intentions. Ask whether they have stuck to their intentions and whether any changes are needed. Ask the team to report examples of when the attitudes have been demonstrated in behaviors and words. Explore how it feels to improve the team attitude and how it feels individually.
7. *Optional Stretch Goal:* Ask the team to create a poster with a thermostat on it and use it before each meeting by asking everyone to check in with his or her level of motivation for the day and how he or she is feeling that day on a scale of 1 to 10. This also supports self-awareness and might be an opportunity for a team member to ask for support, if needed. Then ask each member what level of effectiveness he or she wants the meeting to have that day (1 to 10) and what he or she is willing to personally focus on to move the meeting to that level. Each of these steps builds effective motivation.

Tip

The emotions of the leader are more contagious than the emotions of any other team member. Work individually with the team leader if possible to help him or her recognize this and to exhibit the desired emotional attitude. Guide the team to be aware of how their emotions are affecting their attitude.

ATTITUDE RULES MOTIVATION HANDOUT

"We who lived in concentration camps can remember the men who walked through the huts comforting others, giving away their last pieces of bread. They may have been few in number, but they offer sufficient proof that everything can be taken from a man but one thing: the last of the human freedoms—to choose one's attitude in any given set of circumstances, to choose one's own way." (Frankl, 1992)

Dr. Frankl spent three years at Auschwitz, Dachau, and other concentration camps during World War II. His direct experience is potent and worth taking to heart.

Check in with yourself. How is your attitude at work, with your team, and in other parts of your life?

Discuss and write your answers to these questions on your flip chart:

* What attitudes does the team as a whole choose for meetings, project work, or other engagements?
* Do the attitudes change based on the type of work? If so, how?

Talk with each other about what attitudes you've helped the team develop in the past and what attitudes you want to create in the future.

Reference

Frankl, V. (1959, 1992). *Man's search for meaning* (p. 75). Boston: Beacon Press.

EXERCISE 9.3. FOCUSING ON INSPIRATION

Purpose

To build team motivation by selecting an inspiring project and focusing on it.

Thumbnail

15 to 20 minutes

Team members individually name the most inspiring project on which they are currently working, then select one as a group and create a way to make it visible so they can focus on the motivation it brings.

Outcomes

Team members' motivation will expand as a result of this project, and members will learn ways to keep other motivating projects in mind.

Audience

- Intact teams

Facilitator Competencies

 Easy

Materials

- Flip-chart paper, easel, and markers

Time Matrix

Exercise	Estimated Time
Identify the most inspiring current projects	5 minutes
Facilitate selection of one project by whole team	5 minutes
Post a drawing of the project and keep adding inspiring thoughts	5 to 10 minutes (plus team time to develop drawing)
Total Time	**15 to 20 minutes**

Instructions

1. Go around the room and ask each team member to identify the most inspiring team project in which he or she is currently engaged. Record the ideas on a flip chart.

2. Facilitate a discussion on the options named, eventually guiding the team to choose the one project all team members agree is most inspiring. This is a positive discussion; keep them focused on what works and how to make it even better. Once they identify one project, lead a discussion on why it is inspirational and what they can do to make it even better.

3. In order to keep building the inspiration, instruct the team to find a central location at work, such as a break room, where they can display a large poster or colored drawing of the images and words that make up this inspiring project and that reflect the goal of doing it really well. Ask each team to identify a lead for this poster project to keep them organized and focused and tell them to be sure to meet within a few days so they keep the energy going. Challenge them to keep writing positive items on the drawing to keep the energy and engagement flowing. If possible have follow-up discussions on the project, about how the poster keeps them motivated, and to discuss new ideas. [You are facilitating the strategy at this meeting so they are ready to act afterward.]

Tip

Ask them to be specific about how they will keep the poster or drawing as an engaging focal point.

CHAPTER 10

Team Emotional Awareness

"The amount of attention the team pays to noticing, understanding, and respecting feelings of team members."*

The exercise of team emotional awareness requires members of the team to notice one another's emotions, to seek to understand why the emotions exist when it is relevant to the team engagement, and to respond appropriately. Emotional Awareness is a critical factor in motivation, productivity, and a team's ability to collaborate. It is therefore central to the success of every team; without this vital information, much valuable data is overlooked.

As team members sharpen their skills in emotional awareness, six ingredients will influence success. The ingredients are

---

*M. Hughes & J.B. Terrell. (2009). *Team Emotional and Social Intelligence Facilitator's Guide–TESI® Short*. San Francisco: Pfeiffer.

1. Exploring and using the emotional information received from one another
2. Becoming comfortable with emotions
3. Being aware of a rich assortment of emotional behaviors
4. Discerning the gradations of various emotional responses
5. Being open to others' expression of emotion so one can better understand other team members
6. Gracefully responding, even to emotions of team members that one does not understand or appreciate

Emotions are contagious. Teams whose members effectively perceive, acknowledge, and respond to the emotions of all on the team provide greater opportunity to leverage those emotions in a positive way. Emotions also provide critical data about how successfully a project is progressing and how effective proposed solutions might be. For example, if a team member is eager, frustrated, or worried, others on the team can notice and invite a discussion about those emotions. As team members develop comfort with emotions and compassion in responding to one another, they increase the likelihood of gathering vital information that will enhance the overall team's functioning. This process also increases the chance of building positive relationships and diminishes the possibility of discord. The following three exercises will help build team emotional awareness.

EXERCISE 10.1. NAME THAT EMOTION

Purpose

To expand each team member's ability to recognize emotions experienced by other team members and to express his or her own emotions.

Thumbnail

30 minutes, plus 10 minutes for preparation.

Discuss the importance of team members' ability to identify emotions in themselves and in others. Working in pairs, team members choose slips of paper with emotions written on them. Each member acts out the emotion he or she drew while his or her partner attempts to guess the emotion. The entire team then debriefs the exercise, including ways to continue developing their awareness of and vocabulary for emotions and ways to apply their learnings for the benefit of the team.

Outcomes

Team members will build trust, communication, and conflict-resolution skills by learning how to communicate and respond to key emotional data. They will also improve their effectiveness with key clients and stakeholders.

Audience

- Intact teams
- Individual team members desiring to build skills to take back to the team
- Team leaders

Facilitator Competencies

 Easy

Materials

- Flip-chart paper, easel, and markers
- Slips of paper with emotions written on them

- Container, such as bowl or hat
- Name That Emotion Handout

Time Matrix

Exercise	Estimated Time
In advance, write emotions words on slips of paper	10 minutes
Discuss the value of recognizing emotions	5 minutes
In pairs, act out two emotions and write on flip chart	10 minutes
Discuss experiences and practical applications for team	15 minutes
Total Time	**30 minutes, plus 10 minutes' preparation**

Instructions

1. In advance of the workshop, write emotion words on enough slips of paper for each person to draw two words. Use the list in the handout or any other words desired. Refer to the Appendix for a comprehensive list of feeling words. Put the slips in a container, such as a bowl or a hat.

2. At the workshop, discuss the value of being emotionally aware of one another on the team. Note that there is substantial agreement that nonverbal communication is more accurate than what is said, and a big component of that nonverbal communication is identifying emotional states. Challenge the team to expand their vocabulary of emotional words as well as their skills in understanding one another. Emphasize that it takes skill to effectively communicate one's emotions as well as to read emotional messages from others.

3. Ask the team to break into pairs and then have each person draw two slips of paper out of a hat or other container. Each member of the pair now has two emotion words on slips of paper. One member of each pair engages in a monologue to demonstrate the emotion without using the emotion word. The other member is to identify the emotion reflected in the monologue. Instruct them to keep going until you call time after one minute or until the other person guesses the emotion, whichever

is first. Then the other partner demonstrates an emotion. After each person has completed one word, they should take turns and act out the second word. The purpose is to demonstrate the emotion to a partner without saying it and to go on until the other person names that emotion. When they are finished, ask that they write the four words on a flip-chart page at the front of the room where you have written the word Emotions.

4. Bring the full team back together and ask what they learned and how they expect to be able to use this awareness. Then discuss how to sustain and further develop this awareness. Suggest they keep the flip-chart paper with all the words on a wall somewhere where the team gathers. Encourage them to add to the list whenever someone notices a different emotion to continue building their emotional awareness.

Tip

Connect this with a business purpose for the team. For example, how does it help them to be aware of clients' emotions? This helps build buy-in. Additionally, you might have one pair volunteer to come up front and do the first word in front of everyone. The group is likely to laugh and have fun with the engagement.

NAME THAT EMOTION HANDOUT

This handout is for the facilitator only, not for distribution. Use this or the Appendix to assist your development of the words the team will work with.

Happy
Glad
Excited
Euphoric
Dubious
Worried
Sad
Troubled
Frustrated
Angry
Pensive
Frightened
Exhausted
Drained
Puzzled
Joyous
Hopeful
Apprehensive
Engaged
Tired
Reluctant
Discouraged
Unappreciated
Inquisitive
Bored
Happy
Anxious
Pessimistic
Optimistic
Harried

EXERCISE 10.2. NOTICING EMOTIONS

Purpose

To demonstrate that there are numerous times throughout the day when what is experienced externally and internally has significant effects on attitude, optimism, and motivation.

Thumbnail

30 minutes

Working individually, then in pairs, and then as a whole team, the team members notice their own emotions and talk about them.

Outcomes

Team members will become more aware of emotions experienced individually and within the team. This is one of the first steps in being able to manage individual and team emotions to enhance team effectiveness.

Audience

- Intact teams
- Individual team members desiring to build skills to take back to the team
- Team leaders

Facilitator Competencies

 Easy

Materials

- Noticing Emotions Handout

Time Matrix

Exercise	Estimated Time
Discuss the value of emotional awareness for team	5 minutes
Distribute handout, complete, discuss in pairs	15 minutes
Discuss as whole team	10 minutes
Total Time	**30 minutes**

Instructions

1. Discuss the value of being aware of emotions, personally and across the team. Emotions are fundamental data; recognizing emotions provides opportunities to respond more effectively and to connect better with one another. Tie your discussion to something the team is focused on, such as the importance of being aware of customer emotions, the emotions of other stakeholders, or the emotions of support staff.

2. Distribute the handout to each team member. Ask them to complete it individually and then to pair up with someone to discuss their answers. Tell them they have five minutes to complete the handout and another five minutes for their paired discussions.

3. Bring the full team together and ask for observations. What did they learn about themselves or one another from these fairly straightforward life situations that can occur? How much time do they spend with one another talking about or noticing emotions? How can they strengthen the team by taking even a small amount of time to share something about themselves? How can they strengthen the team by taking time to share or notice how they feel about team projects, deadlines, or other team events?

Tip

Emotional awareness is particularly important for the team leader. You can adapt this exercise and work individually with him or her, as well as with other individual team members.

This can be a good opening exercise in a team training in order to help them connect with their emotions.

NOTICING EMOTIONS HANDOUT

Being sensitive to all the sources of information from the world around you and the world within you is what empowers your behavior with emotional intelligence. The challenge at the team level is to be aware of what you are feeling, where those feelings came from, where they are heading next, *and* to notice the same about your fellow team members.

Emotions are what move and motivate people. Your teammates' emotions influence your emotions, and your emotions influence their emotions. The art of being able to influence your teammates gracefully, enlist their cooperation, and encourage their commitment starts with knowing what you feel and why you feel that way. These skills then expand as you intentionally pay attention to others.

Make a list of the feelings you would likely experience when you place yourself in each of the situations described below. Often there will be more than one feeling.

1. Your whole family has planned a big picnic at the local park. The park does not have any paved areas, but you expect dry weather. You have people coming whom you have not seen in years, even your cousin who is in a wheelchair. Just as everyone arrives and has set up the picnic, a sudden storm starts. Everyone is soaking wet.
2. Your cell phone connection keeps breaking up on an important call.
3. Your favorite TV show is canceled in the middle of the season.
4. You turn on the television and there is a news flash about a suicide bombing.
5. Your manager selects you to explain the value of your team's project to senior leadership.
6. A teacher from your child's school leaves a voicemail message for you to call him as soon as possible.
7. An attractive co-worker asks you out for lunch.
8. You observe a child being treated badly by her angry parent.
9. You win $100 in the lottery.
10. You are waiting for your doctor to review the results of your medical tests.

11. Traffic is very heavy and you miss your exit.
12. For your birthday you receive great tickets to a concert by your favorite band.

There are numerous times throughout the day when what you and your teammates experience externally and internally has significant effects on your attitude, optimism, and motivation. Being aware of these emotional processes is one of the first steps in being able to manage them for yourselves and within your team.

EXERCISE 10.3. PAYING ATTENTION TO US

Purpose

To develop the ability to notice and respond to one another as individuals and thus strengthen the team.

Thumbnail

35 to 45 minutes

Team members discuss as a group the benefits to the team of knowing each other well individually. They then spend a few minutes on their own designing a presentation to the team about individual goals, hobbies, and life learnings. After each individual presentation, team members are encouraged to ask follow-up questions.

Outcomes

As team members learn more about each other, they will communicate better, will manage their emotions and relationships better, will be more collaborative, and will improve team decision making and achievement as a result.

Audience

- Intact teams

Facilitator Competencies

 Easy to Moderate

Materials

- Flip-chart paper, easel, and markers

Time Matrix

Exercise	Estimated Time
Discuss value of emotional awareness	5 minutes
Fill out personal flip-chart pages	10 minutes
Present answers individually	20 to 30 minutes (Adjust according to the size of team)
Total Time	35 to 45 minutes

Instructions

1. Discuss the value the team gains when team members take time to notice one another rather than maintaining a constant focus on just getting the job done. Ask them to itemize specific benefits and record these on a flip chart. Potential ones to name include:
   - Feeling happier
   - Building I've-got-your-back relationships
   - Learning more from one another about the tasks to be done instead of working separately to re-create the wheel
   - Communicating better because they accurately notice and interpret verbal and nonverbal information

2. Guide the team in taking time to tell each other more about themselves. Give each person a sheet of flip-chart paper and ask them to prepare to tell one another about the following:
   - Where they were born
   - A favorite hobby
   - Something really exciting they have learned in life
   - An important goal (it can be about work or personal)

   Give them seven minutes to finish up. Anticipate that there will be many ways of presenting the information. Some will answer the four points in a linear fashion; some are likely to draw a picture.

3. Go around the room and ask each person to present. Allow a few minutes for questions or comments after each presentation to build their ability to get to know one another better.

Developing Emotional and Social Intelligence

4. *Optional Stretch Goal:* Challenge the team to set a time once a month when they will each take a few minutes to talk about something important or interesting to each person individually.

Tip

Keep the discussions and questions safe for everyone. Team members can learn valuable information about each other without being intrusive.

CHAPTER 11

Team Communication

"How well team members listen, encourage participation, and discuss sensitive matters."*

Team communication is the process of sharing information to meet some need or desire in which one part of the team, be it an individual or a subgroup, sends a message that is received by another subgroup or individual team member so that information shared has an impact on the team.

Communication is what team members do to connect with others so that they can understand the collection of goals that are being pursued and how well each is proceeding in the attempt to satisfy all of their needs. Communication is of central importance to every kind of team interaction.

Communication consists of the following components:

- *Sender*: the person who transmits the information
- *Receiver*: the person to whom the information is transmitted

---

**M. Hughes & J.B. Terrell. (2009). *Team Emotional and Social Intelligence Facilitator's Guide–TESI® Short*. San Francisco: Pfeiffer.*

- *Message*: the information transmitted
- *Meaning*: the intent of the message
- *Feeling*: adds depth to the message
- *Technique*: how the message is communicated

Communication is how people interact with one another so they can satisfy their needs and desires to make life better. To communicate, one person (the sender) must transmit information to someone else (the receiver). This message can go to the whole team or to one person, but there has to be an exchange of a message or there is no communication. For example, if a team member speaks about an issue, and another team member later believes he or she never heard of the topic, communication did not occur.

For *effective* communication to occur, the sender's meaning must also be clearly understood by the receiver. Meaning is conveyed by both verbal and nonverbal communication. If the sender's words are encouraging, but he or she is looking down when speaking, the message and meaning are mixed. Nonverbal communication is likely to convey more of the truth, so it is important that the sender's verbal and nonverbal messages be congruent in order for the meaning to be accurately understood.

All communication has meaning, from the trivial—"Please post a notice of our meeting"—to that of huge consequence—"The building is on fire!" The feeling component adds even more depth to the meaning.

Finally, technique is critical for effective communication. Without the awareness and implementation of effective techniques, the message, meaning, and feeling in the communication are lost. The following three exercises will help build team communication.

Developing Emotional and Social Intelligence

EXERCISE 11.1. LISTENING WITH THE EARS OF YOUR HEART

Purpose

To expand team members' understanding of one another and especially to enhance their skills in listening and responding to another team member's entire message—emotions and content.

Thumbnail

50 minutes

The team sets a goal for improving listening and then discusses benefits and barriers to good listening. They engage in an exercise in triads in which they practice observing someone speaking and then the observer repeats the speaker's story. The team discusses what they learned and how they can use their learning to meet the improvement goals they set.

Outcomes

Team members' individual and group communication skills will be improved. In addition, their conflict-resolution skills and ability to build trust will be strengthened.

Audience

- Intact teams
- Individual team members desiring to build skills to take back to the team
- Team leaders

Facilitator Competencies

 Moderate to Advanced

Materials

- Flip-chart paper, easel, and markers
- Pens

- Listening with the Ears of Your Heart Handout 1
- Listening with the Ears of Your Heart Handout 2
- Listening with the Ears of Your Heart Handout 3: Triad Exercise

Time Matrix

Exercise	Estimated Time
Individually assess listening skill levels and record	5 minutes
Discuss benefits and barriers	5 minutes
Complete Triad Exercise	30 minutes
Discuss learning	10 minutes
Total Time	**50 minutes**

Instructions

1. Give everyone a copy of Handout 1. Ask each team member to write down a number representing the quality of their listening as a team. Then write a number that represents their own listening to other team members over the last month. They should choose a number between 1 and 10, with 10 being highest. There will be two numbers: one for their own skill and one for the team's. Then have the team members choose a number that is a reasonable goal for how they would like to rate themselves as well as the team two months from now. Tell them to write their answers on Handout 1.

2. Ask the team about the value of listening. They are likely to have many thoughts, including that it is really important—and that they are not very good at it. Have the team develop a list of why listening is important, and ask them to name the barriers to good listening. After they have created the list, give them Handout 2, which has lists for both areas. Have them discuss their own lists along with the list on the handout for a few minutes.

3. Explain that the purpose of the Triad Exercise is to expand their understanding of one another and to enhance their skills in listening and responding to a team member's entire message—both to emotions

Developing Emotional and Social Intelligence

and to content. Tell them to follow the instructions on Handout 3, the Triad Exercise.

4. Bring the team back together to discuss what they learned. Focus on how they can use their experience to help them improve their listening skills and reach the skill levels they have set as a goal for two months in the future.

Tip

Watch that the observer really puts him- or herself in the position of the speaker when it is time to trade. They should change chairs and the observer should now speak as if he or she is the speaker.

LISTENING WITH THE EARS OF YOUR HEART HANDOUT 1

Current Listening Ability

On a scale of 1 to 10 how good a listener would you
say you are?

Write your answer: _____

On a scale of 1 to 10, how good would you say the team
is at listening?

Write your answer: _____

Desired Listening Ability

On a scale of 1 to 10, how good a listener would you like
to be in two months?

Write your answer: _____

On a scale of 1 to 10, how good would you like the team
to be in two months?

Write your answer: _____

LISTENING WITH THE EARS OF YOUR HEART HANDOUT 2

Value of Good Listening

- Good listening skills make workers more productive.
- The ability to listen carefully will allow you to better understand assignments and what is expected of you.
- Good listening supports building rapport with co-workers, bosses, and clients.
- Listening creates a collaborative spirit and provides a way to show support.
- Good listening enhances skills in resolving challenges with customers, co-workers, and bosses.
- It helps the listener find the underlying meanings in what team members are saying.

Barriers to Effective Listening

- Believing you can multi-task and also think about another matter while listening
- Feelings of bias or prejudice
- Language differences
- Noise
- Worry, fear, or anger
- Poor attention span

LISTENING WITH THE EARS OF YOUR HEART HANDOUT 3: TRIAD EXERCISE

Instructions: You will work in triads. There are three different roles, and each of you will fill each role as you rotate through the exercise three times. The three roles are speaker, listener, and observer. They are described below.

- **Speaker:** Tell the listener about something of moderate importance to you. Be sure to communicate how you feel or felt as you present your story. You do not need to always name the emotion. You may communicate it in many different nonverbal formats. Some of your emotions might be stated out loud, others may be internal. Notice whether the observer picks up on them.
- **Listener:** Listen to the story, noticing the words as well as nonverbal cues. You can comment or talk with the speaker, but keep your comments to a minimum. You are primarily listening. Practice your listening and other communication skills in both the speaker and then the observer scenarios as though you are having a normal conversation.
- **Observer:** Watch and listen to the speaker and the listener carefully.

At the end of three minutes, the speaker finishes. Do not discuss the process. The observer and speaker should trade chairs and the observer should repeat what he or she heard from the speaker. The goal is to match the content and delivery as much as possible. The observer should speak as if he or she is the original speaker, *not as though he or she is talking about the speaker*.

At the end of three minutes, take a few minutes as a group to discuss what you learned and to share tips with each other. The observer should ask the speaker whether he or she captured the essence of the story. Then rotate and repeat the entire process. The Listener is now the Speaker, the Observer is the Listener, and the Speaker is the Observer.

Once you have completed every part of the process, including talking to one another about what you learned the second time, switch roles one more time and repeat the process.

Return to the full group to discuss what you learned and how you can use your experience to help improve your listening skills in your own team.

Developing Emotional and Social Intelligence

EXERCISE 11.2. DIVERSITY MANIA

Purpose

To build awareness of one another's backgrounds and preferences while having fun.

Thumbnail

60 minutes in advance, for facilitator preparation; 25 minutes for the team session

Facilitator sends an email to gather interesting and unique information about the team members and then compiles a handout that the team will use in interacting with each other to find answers to the questions in the handout. They walk around, talk, connect, and have fun while learning.

Outcomes

Team members will learn more about each other so that there is a better connection between them. This will support meeting challenges, managing conflict, and building trust and loyalty. It will also support team identity.

Audience

- Intact teams

Facilitator Competencies

 Easy

Materials

- Diversity Mania Questionnaire—to be created (see sample)
- Diversity Mania Handout—to be created (see sample)
- A prize for the winner

Time Matrix

Exercise	Estimated Time
Compile handout	60 minutes for facilitator only; a few minutes for team members to respond
Team gathers answers to questions on the handout	15 minutes
Discuss results and benefits	10 minutes
Total Time	**60 minutes in advance—facilitator only 25 minutes for the team session**

Instructions

1. In advance of the team session, send out a questionnaire such as the one shown in the sample at the end of this exercise. It should go to every team member via email, with a deadline for response. When you receive the responses, create a twenty-item handout that they will complete during the team exercise. Note: If your team is fewer than six members, ask for more than three responses in order to have enough information for twenty items.

2. At the beginning of the session, tell them to work in groups of two to four, depending on your team size. Distribute the Diversity Mania Handout and tell them they have fifteen minutes to gather the answers to the questions. Say that everyone should stand up, circulate, and talk to other team members.

3. Bring everyone back together, provide the answers, and celebrate the winning group. Then discuss what team members learned. Ask what was the most fun item to learn, the most surprising, and so on. Then guide a discussion on how this type of communication and interaction can make the team stronger.

Tip

Teams that are good at collaborating may come together and answer the questions together. Then they also must collaborate in sharing the prize. Or you may want to have several prizes to reward the benefits of collaboration.

Developing Emotional and Social Intelligence

DIVERSITY MANIA SAMPLE QUESTIONNAIRE

Instructions: This is for the team session of the [name of team] to be held on [date]. Please complete at least three of the items below with something interesting, fun, or informative about you and/or your culture. During the team session, we may ask you to talk about what you write down for a minute or two.

Critical: Email this back to [your name or other facilitator] no later than [time and date].

What is a favorite food of your family/culture and when do you eat it?
Name the design and location of any tattoos or body piercings you have.
Tell us about something unusual that happened to you in childhood.
What month were you born?
Tell us an immigration story that happened to your family.
Tell us a favorite story about a grandparent or other key figure in your life.
You'd never guess I _____ [fill in the blank].
What is your favorite type of music and favorite song?
Tell us anything you want to say that is unique or interesting about you.

Thanks for filling this out and sending it in by [insert time and date]. We're going to put all your answers in a notebook so we you can learn more fun things about each other. Well, you'll see at the team session!

[Facilitator's signature.]

SAMPLE DIVERSITY MANIA HANDOUT

[*Note*: This is a sample of what might be put together from the survey answers. You will need to match the actual answers you have from the survey you do prior to the session.]

Instructions: Circulate, talk to one another, and answer as many of the following questions as possible. There is a prize for finding the most correct answers, especially for getting to know more about each other.

1. Whose favorite singers are Elton John and Stevie Wonder?
2. Whose grandfather played on the girls' baseball team and helped them win by moving up the base?
3. Who loves writing poetry?
4. Whose great grandmother was the first white woman born in [name a city]?
5. Who ate rattlesnake as a child?
6. Who went to private baths with his/her family and for one penny had a private bath?
7. Who caught his/her grandparents skinny dipping?
8. Who ate fried squirrel and squirrel gravy?
9. Who has over one hundred cousins?
10. Who received last rites three times as a child?
11. Whose father has American Indian ancestry?
12. Who got in trouble for climbing on the roof of his/her school as a child?
13. Who has a scar on his/her eyebrow in the same exact place as his/her uncle and grandfather have?
14. Who has a tattoo? What is it? Where is it?
15. Whose great, great grandfather survived a wagon train attack?
16. Whose mom's cooking was the strangest thing he/she ate as a child?
17. Who has mixed heritage—Irish and English?
18. Who received a scholarship for eight consecutive years?
19. Who loves Lucy (the cartoon character)?
20. Who was stranded in the Peruvian Andes after a train wreck?

EXERCISE 11.3. TURN OFF EMAIL!

Purpose

To create ways to break the habit of indirect email communication between team members and increase face-to-face communication.

Thumbnail

30 to 35 minutes in session; 15 to 30 minutes weekly after session

Team members discuss challenges preventing face-to-face communication and develop a strategy to enhance it, including a commitment to refrain from internal emails for one-half to one full day per week for a month. Members create compliance incentives and review each other's brief reports each week to encourage and measure their progress.

Outcomes

Team members will develop a sustainable communication enhancement strategy that causes them to talk with one another directly, thus building understanding, emotional awareness, and relationships.

Audience

- Intact teams
- Individual team members desiring to build skills to take back to the team
- Team leaders

Facilitator Competencies

 Easy

Materials

- Flip-chart paper, easel, and markers

Time Matrix

Exercise	Estimated Time
Discuss challenges to communication	10 minutes
Commit to not email	10 to 15 minutes
Create compliance incentives	10 minutes
Review reports weekly	15 to 30 minutes weekly
Total Time	**30 to 35 minutes in session;** **15 to 30 minutes weekly**

Instructions

1. Discuss with the team that face-to-face communication is increasingly challenged and ask them to list the reasons why. Be sure they tell the truth that sometimes they hide behind an email rather than deal with challenges face-to-face. Record their reasons on a flip chart. Divide your flip-chart page to list Barriers to Communication on one side and Possible Responses on the other. Discuss the emotional concerns about directly communicating with one another. Give team members a chance to thoroughly talk through their feelings and resistance as well as excitement about a new strategy.

2. Have them commit to a radical response—turning off internal email between team members for one-half day to one full day per week for a month. Have them commit to standing up and talking to one another or picking up the phone if the distance is too far to visit face-to-face. Create specific agreements and write them on the flip chart with a promise to give everyone a copy after the session. This should be labeled the Team Communication Enhancement Strategy and might read like the one below.

Team Communications Enhancement Strategy

Team X and all of its members hereby agree to implement the following:

- We will **not** email one another every Thursday morning from October 1 to October 31.
- Each of us will talk face-to-face with team members at least X times that morning.

- For those team members who are too far away for us to walk to their desks, which means they are X far away, each of us will make at least X calls to them.
- Each of us will fill out a quick memo every Thursday for this month with the list of people we went to see or called on Thursday mornings. We will bring our reports to the next weekly team meeting and discuss progress and any potential new strategies.

3. Challenge the team to create compliance incentives. Perhaps the people with the most face-to-face interactions each week would receive a small prize. What is recognized and rewarded is repeated. Guide the team to evaluate their commitment to a long-term agreement to enhancing their communication so that they take this beyond a short-term intervention.

4. Review each person's report at weekly meetings throughout the month.

5. *Optional Stretch Goal:* Meet with the team regularly during the month and then quarterly to review their actions and learnings and to build their practice of direct communication into a long-term sustainable approach. Guide them to develop a strategy to bring new team members to understand and practice this approach.

Tip

Watch for those who seek to get around the rule by writing many emails and then just sending the emails after the deadline. Ask the team whether they want to create a way to catch this avoidance behavior. Commitment from the team leader is essential for this to be effective. Some may object that emails are needed to confirm specific documentation. Agree and suggest that those be done during the rest of the week. This is a deliberate action intervention intended to deal with a serious issue of team members not talking to one another.

CHAPTER 12

Team Stress Tolerance

*"How well the team is managing the pressures of work load, time constraints, and the real needs for work-life balance."**

Stress tolerance is the skill of holding the world's parade of unpleasant surprises at bay. The scale most closely linked to physical health, stress tolerance is the ability to work with the right amount of creative tension without letting it go too far, running your life and ruining your health.

Team members significantly influence one another's stress levels. Together, members can form effective strategies for tolerating an appropriate level of stress and for changing circumstances if the demands become too much. This reflects the team's ability to understand the types of stress factors and the intensity impacting others and the team as a whole.

As demands on the workforce increase daily, team members need to pay even more attention to developing skills to manage expectations so those demands don't take a toll on

---

*M. Hughes & J.B. Terrell. (2009). *Team Emotional and Social Intelligence Facilitator's Guide–TESI® Short*. San Francisco: Pfeiffer.

health or happiness. What many team members don't realize is how much they can help one another in managing stress. A team can do so through stress-releasing activities for the whole team, such as group stretching or brief relaxation sessions. They can also be good role models for one another, for example, by taking the stairs instead of the elevator or by limiting unnecessary emails.

The seven ingredients that compose stress tolerance are

1. *Environmental awareness:* This includes both physical and emotional components
2. *Assertiveness:* Taking steps to protect oneself from the impacts of stress
3. *Self-regard:* Thinking enough of oneself to believe stress relief is deserved
4. *Wellness:* An expanding sense of work/life balance
5. *Humor:* As stress management improves, so does one's sense of humor, which has a positive impact at work
6. *Flexibility:* The ability to realistically assess the importance of a project and to consider alternative ways to address it
7. *Humility:* This helps slow the pace and show more compassion for teammates

Teams manage their stress tolerance by being aware of the environment—the entire environment, including the physical components as well as the emotional ones. Are people tense or at ease? Are they comfortable in the setting? If not, what might shift the tension? These questions demonstrate the importance of assertiveness (to protect from the impacts of stress) and self-regard (to believe that stress relief is deserved). When individual team members and the team as a whole develop stress tolerance, everyone's experience of wellness will include an expanding sense of work/life balance. Humor will improve and begin to lighten up the atmosphere at work and at home.

Just how important is that project? Will it make a worldwide difference? Will it matter in several weeks or several years? Flexibility supports stress tolerance because it helps team members be sufficiently resilient to find a variety of answers. Adding a dose of humility can help the team members slow down and be more compassionate with each other. Being able to find a workaround when it seems as though the team is stuck can make the difference between completing the project and leaving it undone. The following three exercises will help build team stress tolerance.

EXERCISE 12.1. WORK AND PLAY

Purpose

To support one another in gaining perspective regarding what is considered a healthy amount of time to spend at work.

Thumbnail

10 minutes in advance; 65 minutes in session

The team members talk about non-work activities that they enjoy and present symbols of these activities to help bring them to life. Then the team develops a plan to actively support work/life balance.

Outcomes

Team members will support one another in enhancing work/life balance. This exercise will also strengthen team identity as they will get to know more about each other. Team motivation and positive mood are also likely to be enhanced.

Audience

- Intact teams

Facilitator Competencies

 Moderate

Materials

- Flip-chart paper, easel, and markers

Time Matrix

Exercise	Estimated Time
Team members collect symbols of pleasurable non-work activities	10 minutes per person
Discuss the value of work/life balance and of supporting one another	10 minutes
Show and discuss the symbols	5 minutes per person
Develop a team strategy	15 minutes
Check out the plan and finalize	10 minutes
Total Time	**10 minutes in advance; 65 minutes in session (or more for teams with more than six members)**

Instructions

1. In advance of the session, ask team members to gather three or more symbols of what they enjoy outside of work. Encourage them to include something representing a minimum of three different activities. The symbols can be a baseball, ballet shoes, pictures, a yoga mat, and so on.

2. At the beginning of the session, explain that activities other than work are valuable and emphasize that each person on the team should take time to engage in other enjoyable activities. Further, team members should support one another in this effort. This can help them keep the amount of time they spend at work in healthy proportion to who they are as whole people. Creativity studies and neurological research show that when we're rested and feel fulfilled by diversity in our lives, we are more pleasant, more creative, and more productive. Ironically, spending less time at work can result in an output similar to that of a team that works more hours. Additionally, creativity may well be higher. However, the "to do" list generated by the numerous tasks and expectations at work can seem so compelling that it's hard to pull away. Therefore, taking time to learn about one another's interests helps team

members support each other in breaking the hypnotic trance of task orientation. Engage the team in this discussion.

3. Invite the team members to show their symbols to one another and to each make a few comments about why they enjoy the particular activity symbolized. This can be done with the whole team if the team is small enough. Otherwise, have them break into small groups.

4. Ask the team to develop a strategy they could adopt for supporting one another in finding a good balance. For example:

   - They can take thirty minutes a month to discuss other interests.
   - They can ask each other what is happening in their interest areas during the day when the opportunity arises. A brief conversation can be a power break that refreshes the person when he or she goes back to the work of the day.
   - If some share common interests, they can participate together—be it yoga, baseball games, or hiking.

5. Once the strategy is drafted, help the team apply reality testing. Check whether it will really be implemented and how they will know it is successful. Discuss challenges. The purpose is to create a solid and enduring plan. Explore how getting some time to talk about outside activities feels and how it supports productivity.

6. *Optional Stretch Goal:* Set a meeting in a month to review progress and success. Be willing to make adjustments to the plan if necessary.

Tip

If there is resistance from some because "this isn't work-related" from their perspective, let them discuss their concerns. Ask others to talk about how taking a break helps them work better or make similar points. Don't push. If some are hesitant, perhaps they can watch the team develop and join in as they are comfortable.

EXERCISE 12.2. WHEN THE INTERNET IS DOWN

Purpose

To help teams identify effective approaches for managing stress and negative emotions during times of change and unpredictability.

Thumbnail

35 to 50 minutes

Team members divide into smaller groups, are given a stress-producing scenario, and are asked to create an emergency response plan that they later share with the entire team. The scenario is that Internet access has been lost for the rest of the day, with a major Internet-dependent project due the following day. As they present their emergency plans to each other, members are asked to generalize their approaches to other stressful situations in which they might be forced to create an environment that encourages the most effective possible response to unpredictability.

Outcomes

Team members will develop a variety of emotional intelligence skills as they work together to create an emergency plan. As they debrief their plans later, they will also gain insights into general approaches that are effective in managing stress, which will help them function more effectively during times of organizational change.

Audience

- Intact teams

Facilitator Competencies

 Moderate

Materials

- Flip-chart paper, easel, and markers

Time Matrix

Exercise	Estimated Time
Discuss examples of challenging and surprising events	5 to 10 minutes
Discuss pros and cons	5 to 10 minutes
Create emergency response teams	15 minutes
Present plans and develop strategies for stress responses	10 to 15 minutes
Total Time	**35 to 50 minutes**

Instructions

1. Discuss with the team what happens when a core part of their work life is significantly disrupted, such as the Internet going down. Ask them to talk about experiences with this team or other teams where this or similar scenarios have happened and encourage them to fully consider how the teams responded.

2. Make a list of the responses teams made on a flip chart and discuss pros and cons of those responses.

3. Ask the team to divide into groups of three or four and give each group a flip-chart page and markers. Tell them they will have twelve and a half minutes to respond to the scenario you will read to them and that they will be presenting their plans to the entire team at the end. Each group is to consider themselves as the emergency response team that's in charge of maintaining a positive attitude, keeping stress levels in check, and getting work done. *Note:* The unusual time of twelve and a half minutes is because unusual times command better attention and helps maintain the sense that this isn't business as normal.

Scenario

The whole team is at work in the morning, you're getting some big projects out, and productivity is good. You have a big deadline that is heavily dependent on having an Internet connection. Just as work is going at a good buzz, the Internet goes down! Really out—truly down; neither computers nor phones can access the Internet or receive email. And the word is it won't be back up until evening. Administration has stipulated that no one can leave; they must stay on site until the normal end of the work day, which means about six more hours of work.

4. Instruct groups to write "Emergency Response Team Plan" at the top of their flip-chart pages and then to list the key components of their action plans. Explain that their plans must include all the actions, behaviors, and attitudes they want team members to embrace in order to meet the goals of maintaining a positive attitude, keeping stress levels in check, and accomplishing the work. If you need to suggest ideas as the teams work on their plans, some possible items to include are:
   - Take a half-hour and play just to lighten things up—could be cards, monopoly, or basketball (can't be computer games!!).
   - Get together and have everyone write down ideas, even if a bit silly, about how the Internet going down is good for them.
   - Talk to members of the team and make a list of what other projects need to be done but just haven't received attention because the Internet work has always come first. This might be so humble as to clean up the office and file, but just imagine how great the office will look and how welcoming it will be!
   - Engage in some physical stress-reduction strategies such as breathing, sitting quietly for a few minutes, or eating chocolate!

5. When time is up, ask each Emergency Response Team to present their plan and to discuss it with the goal of increasing awareness of how to manage stress in trying times.

Tip

This scenario or others like it that interfere with the expected activities of the day are very likely to happen from time to time. The team can be thrown off center with members becoming upset and angry, with the result that it's a lost day or, even worse, by influencing the team with a negative attitude. The idea behind this exercise is to take charge of the unusual situation and make it a golden opportunity. People who live where it snows will recognize this as being similar to getting a "snow day" at work, a day when people largely stay home because it's not wise or possible to drive. The world becomes quieter, more peaceful, and is quite refreshing. Encourage the team to build inspiring responses to surprising challenges. They are in charge of their attitudes.

EXERCISE 12.3. ENERGIZERS AND STRESS TRIGGERS

Purpose

To understand which behaviors bring energy to the team and which behaviors trigger stressful responses so that team members can replicate healthy, energizing behaviors and minimize stressful behaviors that have a negative impact on the team.

Thumbnail

40 to 55 minutes

Team members identify and explore specific behaviors that energize the team. Then the individual members consider team behaviors that trigger stress responses and suggest more positive behaviors when sharing with the rest of the team.

Outcomes

The team's stress tolerance will be enhanced when team members become aware of the level and elements of team stress they can control. Once they identify the behaviors that most energize the team, members can make more informed choices to continue these behaviors. This also leads to a more resilient team and the creation of a climate of increased positive mood.

Audience

- Intact teams
- Individual team members desiring to build skills to take back to the team
- Team leaders

Facilitator Competencies

 Moderate

Materials

- Flip-chart paper, easel, and markers
- Energizers and Stress Triggers Handout

Time Matrix

Exercise	Estimated Time
Create lists of energizers and stress triggers	5 to 10 minutes
Discussion	5 to 10 minutes
Share energizer behaviors, identify patterns, and create strategies	10 minutes
Consider stress triggers and generate ideas for improved behaviors	5 to 10 minutes
Facilitate discussion	10 minutes
Discussion of positive impacts on team	5 minutes
Total Time	**40 to 55 minutes**

Instructions

1. Distribute the Energizers and Stress Triggers Handout. Ask team members to work individually to identify three specific behaviors that the team engages in or could engage in that would enhance team energy and positive working relationships and to write those in the Energizers column on the handout. Then have team members identify three specific team behaviors that trigger a stress response and detract from a positive work environment. Have them list these in the Stress Triggers column. Tell them that they will be sharing their energizers with the team, but it is their choice whether to share their stress triggers.

2. Lead a discussion about the importance of creating a work environment with enough stress to work with creative tension, yet not be debilitating by tolerating inappropriate levels of stress. Ask the team to engage in a conversation answering questions such as:

   • What kind of a work environment allows us as team members to deal with stress in a productive manner?

   • What kind of a work environment contributes to intolerable levels of stress for us?

3. Have all team members share their energizer behaviors. Write these behaviors on a flip chart entitled Individual Energizers.

4. Once all behaviors have been captured, ask the team members to consider patterns of energizing behaviors from the entire list. Identify and discuss words energizers on which there is considerable agreement and those that could serve the whole team. Write those on a flip-chart page entitled Team Energizers.

5. Guide the team to identify strategies that will promote and enhance energizer behaviors for the ongoing wellness of team members. Ask, "What are two or three ways of interacting that would reinforce and enhance these behaviors on this team?" Record these ideas on a flip chart labeled Team Improved Behaviors.

6. Now ask the team members to privately review their list of stress triggers. Ask them to consider what effective individual or team behavior would minimize each trigger and write that in the Suggested Improved Behaviors column on their handouts. For example, if they wrote, "last-minute demands" in their Stress Trigger column, they can suggest, "enough lead time on assignments to do the job well." Ask for feedback on what team members wrote for stress triggers as well as improved behaviors. Encourage an open environment in which team members share without judgment or ridicule.

7. Ask team members to discuss how to implement any of the suggested behaviors to enhance the team's effectiveness and reduce stress.

8. *Optional Stretch Goal:* You might also ask the team to identify events where stress could help the team perform. For example, tight deadlines can be stress triggers. They can also motivate a team to push for action and create urgency, which can actually help a team pull together during tough times. You might ask: "What are two or three ways of interacting that might increase stress in a positive way if we do not overdo the strategy?"

Tip

Encourage team members to write new ideas on their handouts to remind them which behaviors are most effective and encouraged.

ENERGIZERS AND STRESS TRIGGERS HANDOUT

	Energizers	Stress Triggers	Suggested Improved Behaviors
1.			
2.			
3.			

More ideas for improved behaviors:

CHAPTER 13

Team Conflict Resolution

"How constructively the team conducts the process of disagreement and whether the team is able to deal with adversity to enhance its functioning, rather than being caught up in the conflict."*

Team conflict occurs when there is disagreement based on different perspectives, values, or priorities that rises to the level of disrupting the effective team system. Conflict resolution is the process followed by the individuals and teams who are facing such a challenge. Many styles of resolution can be engaged, including cooperation, confrontation, competition, and the most sophisticated—collaboration. Managing conflict and taking advantage of the awareness it can bring is essential for team productivity and creativity.

People learn and grow through conflict. Any change will include some aspect of conflict. However, when the change is easy or welcome, it is seldom seen as a conflict. Only when there is dispute, disagreement, or dissatisfaction is a change

---

*M. Hughes & J.B. Terrell. (2009). *Team Emotional and Social Intelligence Facilitator's Guide–TESI® Short*. San Francisco: Pfeiffer.

viewed as conflict. The way team members respond to conflict has a significant impact on the team's effectiveness. If some members of the team, especially the team leader, are conflict-averse and shy away from dealing with issues, it can undermine the team. Pretending an issue is not there will not make it disappear. In fact, this can escalate a problem situation, as it might encourage passive-aggressive and other less transparent behaviors that interfere with a team accomplishing its mission. No matter how much team members fear conflict, they can build their skills in learning how to face and respond to conflict in ways that ultimately benefit the team.

The ingredients for resolving conflict include the following:

- Patience/willingness
- Perspective
- Intention/attention
- Collaborative communications
- Empathy
- Assertiveness
- Choice in conflict resolution style
- Humor
- Gratitude

Resolving conflict begins with *patience* and the *willingness* to engage and to listen. Effective conflict resolution requires having an *intention* to solve key issues and then paying *attention* to what is critical to achieving a solution. Teams that are able to solve problems recognize that each member brings a different *perspective* to the matter and use *collaborative communication* strategies to solve them. Such communication strategies require an artful combination of being *assertive* while also showing *empathy* for one another. Teams benefit by understanding that there are many ways to deal with conflict so they can make good *choices* about how to address difficult matters, from the mundane to the critical. A sense of *humor* helps team members not take themselves or any problem too seriously; it helps open team members' thinking and their ability to recognize the possibilities of different solutions. Finally, *gratitude* helps highlight what the team has done well, which can motivate members toward even more effective conflict resolution efforts in the future. The following three exercises will help build team conflict resolution skills.

EXERCISE 13.1. SWOT YOUR TEAM CONFLICT

Purpose

To build awareness among the team members about the conflict resolution approach the team uses and to establish strategic goals for improvement.

Thumbnail

65 to 70 minutes

The team learns about the SWOT (strengths, weaknesses, opportunities, and threats) process, and then each individual fills out the handout, completing a SWOT analysis on a past conflict the team has encountered. As a whole, the team discusses potential components for each of the four SWOT categories and develops a plan to apply in future conflict scenarios.

Outcomes

Team members will enhance their conflict resolution skills by learning to apply the structured SWOT process to evaluate their current approach to conflict resolution. With this information, they will then establish a strategy to improve their team's conflict resolution approach.

Audience

- Intact teams

Facilitator Competencies

 Moderate

Materials

- Flip-chart paper, easel, and markers
- Paper
- SWOT Your Team Conflict Handout

Time Matrix

Exercise	Estimated Time
Discuss SWOT process and team's conflict resolution process	10 minutes
Fill out handout	15 minutes
List scenarios team members wrote about	5 minutes
Identify strengths and weaknesses the team used on one conflict	10 minutes
Identify opportunities and threats	10 minutes
Identify other key ideas, develop a plan of action	15 to 20 minutes
Total Time	**65 to 70 minutes**

Instructions

1. Discuss the SWOT process with the team. Explain that the acronym stands for Strengths, Weaknesses, Opportunities, and Threats. Explain the purpose and process they will use during this exercise. Applying this process creates a strategic format for the team to consider how effectively they resolve conflict. They will discuss strengths and weaknesses they notice from previous times the team has solved conflicts and then identify opportunities for improvement. They will seek to spot threats to accomplishing those opportunities. They will discuss how to use their emotional engagement more effectively.

2. Give each team member the SWOT Your Team Conflict Handout. Ask people to work individually and take fifteen minutes to identify a specific conflict the team encountered and then answer the questions about that decision-making process. *Tip*: If they have trouble thinking of scenarios on their own, you can have the team as a whole brainstorm a list of conflicts with which they have dealt. It will be good to generate four or more scenarios. Be very careful to not let them problem solve the process at this stage. Reconvene the team and open the discussion by asking what scenarios were chosen. Write a summary title for each

Developing Emotional and Social Intelligence

scenario named on a flip chart. Then ask the team to choose one scenario to discuss in more detail.

3. Invite discussion on the strengths and weaknesses and emotions the team employed in addressing the conflict scenario chosen. Those who identified this scenario in their handout notes will be able to start the conversation. Write headings of Strengths, Weaknesses, Opportunities, and Threats on a flip chart. Write down central points that are made under each of the strength and weakness areas as they are discussed.

4. Now ask what opportunities exist for the team to improve their conflict resolution process as demonstrated by this scenario. Note that they are just brainstorming at this time, and encourage creative discussion. However, do guide the discussion to concrete examples that can be implemented. Ask them to choose a few specific actions from the brainstormed list. Then ask what threats exist to the likelihood of implementing these opportunities. For example, they may feel too much pressure to feel comfortable taking time to be deliberative. Encourage a full conversation about how the threats might be managed to allow the opportunity to be implemented and how they can use their emotional engagement with one another more effectively. Again, write key points under opportunities and threats on the flip chart.

5. Ask what other ideas they listed on the handout for other scenarios. List key ideas presented in each of the categories. Then create a strategic plan for enhancing the team conflict resolution process. Go through each of the four areas, beginning with strengths, and have them select the items that will go in the final plan. Keep the team focused on the process rather than becoming side-tracked by seeking to resolve a particular matter. Consistently discuss their emotional engagement in each stage.

Tip

Team members are likely to feel tempted to solve issues they are discussing or to become lost in debating details. Keep reminding the team that now is the time to take a higher-level view and that, once the process is in place, they will be able to do a better job in resolving future challenges. Include discussions of how this process can also help them be aware of one another's emotions. Exercise 5.3, Decision Making, Emotions, and Thinking Styles, is a great complement to this exercise.

SWOT YOUR TEAM CONFLICT HANDOUT

Instructions: Identify a real situation in which the team needed to resolve or work with a conflict. Then answer the following questions about it.

- What were the team's STRENGTHS in solving the conflict? What emotional engagement in the team supports those strengths?

- What were the team's WEAKNESSES in solving the conflict? What emotional engagement in the team leads to those weaknesses?

- What OPPORTUNITIES can you now see that the team had to improve its resolution of this conflict? What emotional engagement in the team makes these opportunities feasible?

- Should the team decide to use those opportunities in resolving future conflicts, what THREATS exist to the successful use of those new strategies? What emotional engagement in the team should be noticed to manage these threats?

EXERCISE 13.2. JUDGING OR OPEN-MINDED?

Purpose

To expand awareness of negative energy and judging oneself or others in order to improve the conflict resolution process.

Thumbnail

50 minutes

Team members discuss the consequences of negative emotions on individuals and on the team conflict resolution process, learn a strategy for releasing the negative emotions, and set a strategy for future open-minded decisions individually and as a team.

Outcomes

Team members will develop new skills for becoming less judgmental, more creative, and more effective at resolving conflict. They learn a strategy for releasing judgment and other negative emotions and set a strategy for resolving future conflicts with open-minded creativity.

Audience

- Intact teams
- Individual team members desiring to build skills to take back to the team
- Team leaders

Facilitator Competencies

 Moderate

Materials

- Flip-chart paper, easel, and markers
- Pens
- Judging or Open-Minded? Handout

Time Matrix

Exercise	Estimated Time
Discuss the impacts of negative energy	10 minutes
Fill in first two parts of the handout individually	5 minutes
Discuss handout in pairs	10 minutes
Whole team discussion	5 minutes
Guided process to let go of the negative energy	5 minutes
Finish handout	5 minutes
Establish team strategy	10 minutes
Total Time	**50 minutes**

Instructions

1. Guide the team in discussing the impacts personally as well as to one another of being judgmental of themselves or of others. Explain that team members can be emotionally derailed by strong negative feelings and judgments of themselves or one another. Once a person becomes upset, the natural tendency is to seek to project that difficult emotion onto someone else in order to get it out of one's system. This projection is often expressed as a judgment of what you or someone else has done wrong. If the difficult energy isn't placed on someone else, the likely result will be to blame yourself. Either form of blaming is a toxic response that is likely to backfire. It will hold the individual up by backing up the free flow of energy and becoming a drain on resources. It limits creativity and leads to poor decisions. Furthermore, judging others leads to blocking the ability to receive their information, thus lessening the pool of data from which the team can draw while problem solving. Note that some of the consequences can be personal angst, frustration, and increased stress, as well as poorer decisions.

2. Instruct the team members to individually fill out the first two parts of the handout, identifying a time when they were judgmental and another time when they managed to convert the tendency to being

Developing Emotional and Social Intelligence

judgmental by being open-minded. Ask them to seek to identify what supported the ability to be open-minded in the second situation.

3. Ask them to form pairs and to discuss what they wrote.
4. Reconvene the whole team and discuss:
   - The costs of being judgmental;
   - The benefits of being open-minded
   - How to manage the temptation to be judgmental
5. Guide the team in a process to transform the toxic negative energy in order to release the temptation to be judgmental by following these steps. Ask them to:
   - Put down anything they are holding and put their feet on the floor and sit in a relaxed upright position.
   - Take a deep breath and let it out slowly. Keep focusing on their breathing, letting go of the troubling thoughts, and just focusing on the breathing.
   - Continue until they feel their energy relaxing and you say to stop.
6. Gradually bring them back to the room and ask team members to return to their handouts and individually take notes on their personal open-minded strategies.
7. Bring the team together to establish team goals of supporting one another in an open-minded and creative approach to conflict resolution.

Tip

The individual and team open-minded strategies should be as specific as possible in order to create an actionable plan.

JUDGING OR OPEN-MINDED? HANDOUT

Instructions:

1. Identify a time when you were judgmental of yourself or others during a team conflict, and then another time that you managed to convert the tendency to being judgmental to being open-minded. Identify what supported the ability to be open-minded in the second situation.

2. Note how your emotions lead you to being judgmental and then how you feel after you have formed or expressed your judgments. What were the emotional consequences of being judgmental as compared to being open minded?

■ ■ ■

After the team discussion, complete the following:

3. Describe the strategies you will follow in the future to be more open-minded.

EXERCISE 13.3. TO CONFRONT OR NOT TO CONFRONT

Purpose

To provide team members an opportunity to practice new conflict resolution skills and to identify effective techniques for moving past an impasse.

Thumbnail

50 minutes

Participants discuss the role of anger and conflict in team effectiveness. They then divide into pairs and take turns playing two roles: someone eager to accept a new project and someone resisting it. They debrief in pairs after each role play, share their learnings with the full group, and identify new strategies for managing team conflict in the future.

Outcomes

Team members will develop conflict resolution skills as well as an understanding of when confrontation is appropriate and when other conflict resolution skills are more effective.

Audience

- Individuals in group training
- Intact teams

Facilitator Competencies

 Moderate to Advanced

Materials

- Flip-chart paper, easel, and markers
- To Confront or Not to Confront Handout

Time Matrix

Exercise	Estimated Time
Discuss impact of anger and impasse on team effectiveness	10 minutes
Guide identification and discussion	10 minutes
Role plays and debriefings	20 minutes
Complete their strategy	10 minutes
Total Time	**50 minutes**

Instructions

1. Aristotle is frequently quoted as saying: "Anyone can become angry—that is easy. But to be angry with the right person, to the right degree, at the right time, for the right purpose, and in the right way; this is not easy." Refer to the quote and ask questions such as:
   - When is it useful to express anger? When is expressing anger a mistake? Why?
   - What experiences have you had that support your responses to the first questions?
   - What is the role that expressing anger has in supporting effective conflict resolution?
2. Lead a discussion on the role of anger in the effectiveness of teamwork. One of the ways anger is expressed is through confrontation between two or more people. Ask questions such as the following and take notes on the flip chart as relevant points are raised or comments are stated that reflect or challenge team norms.
   - What does confrontation mean to you?
   - What are potential risks and benefits to confronting someone?
   - What emotions come up for you when you are confrontational?
   - Impasse is a point at which no further progress can be made or agreement reached. When have you experienced confrontation leading to impasse?
   - Are there different terms or concepts that better describe ways to deal with an issue so that the disagreement and the worry are addressed

Developing Emotional and Social Intelligence

without being confrontational? What are those ways? Discuss them in detail.

3. Guide the participants to discuss how they resolve conflict. Ask for specific examples and details so they become aware of current practices that may be unconscious habitual behaviors. If the team or group is large, break them into small groups to first conduct the discussion and then come back to the group as a whole with their responses. Look for points to be made such as:

   - Anger is a reflection that early signs of conflict or difficulties were not dealt with. When something festers, it gets worse. Thus, one of the team goals can be to become more proactive in addressing mild disagreements or challenges.

   - Anger can also be an indication that someone feels misunderstood and possibly hurt. People may argue over content when the real issue may be about process. Confrontation does not always have to be forceful. Sometimes gently raising an awareness of the other person's emotions—noting that he or she might be feeling frustrated or disrespected, for example—can shift the interaction past impasse.

   - One of the consequences of anger is that stress for all involved escalates, and that leads to more mistakes. This is a foundational concern, as it is probably a mistake or someone's perception that a mistake occurred that led to the anger in the first place.

4. Tell the participants that they are going to conduct a role play that puts them in the position of deciding whether to be confrontational and if so how they will do so. Divide them into pairs. Note that the full group will be discussing the learning and recognitions following the role play. As the facilitator, feel free to change the nature of the challenge from rewriting the policy manual to a task more relevant to this team. Give them the handout with the role play and tell them each person is to play both roles. In Round 1 they are to decide who plays which role and take seven minutes to conduct the role play, followed by three minutes to debrief in their pair. Then change roles and take the same time again for Round 2.

5. Bring the full group back together for a discussion on what they learned. Ask them to revisit the discussion on how they work with anger and confrontation. Now that they have experienced a difficult

situation, ask them to set an intention and strategy for how they will work with these challenging situations in the future.

Tip

Make this a thoughtful learning environment and be sure they stay considerate and respectful of divergent views throughout the exercise. As the facilitator, help the group discuss the emotions they encountered in each scenario and how they managed those emotions, as well as the techniques they used to deal with the impasse.

TO CONFRONT OR NOT TO CONFRONT HANDOUT

Instructions: You should each play both roles. In Round 1 decide who plays which role and take seven minutes to conduct the role play, followed by three minutes to debrief. Then change roles and take the same time again for a second round.

Overview

This is a role play in which you experience the challenge of starting at what looks like a firm impasse and then take on the challenge of moving from the point of being stuck to an active engagement. It's a classic situation of seeking to move from no to yes. In the two-person role play, one person, Jean, is at an impasse. S/he feels that no is the only right answer to the boss's request for a new project to be completed within a tight deadline. Jean has a lot of other feelings as well. Notice what they are, do your best to respond effectively, and be prepared to talk about the feelings and responses when the full group debriefs.

Terry wants to accept the new assignment and is challenged with persuading Jean to get on board. Should Terry confront Jean? This will be one of the elements that you choose as you conduct this role play. Terry is feeling that saying yes to the boss is the only right answer. Terry has many other feelings as well. Notice what they are, do your best to respond effectively, and be prepared to talk about the feelings and responses when the full group debriefs.

Role for Person A: Jean

Jean is so angry. S/he is part of a team that has just been handed a new assignment to rewrite the company's entire policy manual. The job is supposed to be done by next Monday, and there's no way it can be done in time. S/he was going to finish two other key jobs this week and now this—and s/he's secretly scared. They don't have enough data or time to make the anticipated revisions and s/he doesn't want to look foolish.

Role for Person B: Terry

Terry is also concerned with the timeline. But the boss set the deadline and is inflexible on this one. Terry needs Jean's help. S/he's really great when s/he wants to contribute.

CHAPTER

14

Team Positive Mood

"The level of encouragement, sense of humor, and how successful the team expects to be."*

Happiness and *optimism* are aspects of having a positive mood and are vital parts of emotional and social intelligence. Happiness is based on one's ability to be satisfied with what happens today. It reflects the ability to accept all that is here right now, embrace it, and be deeply grateful. Optimism is the team and team members' hopefulness about future outcomes. It is embodied in part by a team's can-do attitude, an attitude that energizes all successful teams. Happiness and optimism enhance the level of encouragement present, including members' sense of humor and how successful the team expects to be. These attributes are the major support for a team's flexibility and resilience.

---

*M. Hughes & J.B. Terrell. (2009). *Team Emotional and Social Intelligence Facilitator's Guide–TESI® Short*. San Francisco: Pfeiffer.

The seven ingredients of a team's positive mood are

1. Positive/can-do attitude
2. Hopefulness
3. Curiosity
4. Long-term view (perspective)
5. Attitude of abundance, a sense that good things are going to happen for the team
6. Playfulness
7. Zest

Positive attitude, often referred to as a "can-do" attitude, is a strong indicator of optimism. It helps team members believe that they can find successful and effective solutions to challenges. A team with a strong positive mood will be *hopeful* about the future and grateful for what is going well today. The members will reflect a sense of *curiosity* about what else is possible. When big challenges arise, they will take the *long-term view* that builds perspective. Teams that have strength in positive mood have a *sense of abundance*—that good things happen to them. They will encourage *playfulness* in one another, and all of these skills build a sense of *zest* for the projects on the table and the possibilities in the future. The following three exercises will help build positive team mood.

EXERCISE 14.1. CULTURAL FEST

Purpose

To encourage team members to share more about their cultural experiences so they learn and appreciate more about each other, which leads to stronger team functioning.

Thumbnail

2 hours over three meetings (depending on team size and specific needs)

Team members are first asked to plan a team event at which each member will present something about his or her culture. Each presentation will include an action—eating, dancing, playing a musical instrument or game, for example—and a story that accompanies the action. The second meeting is the event itself, and the third meeting—no more than one week later—is a time to debrief and explore the emotional impact of the event.

Outcomes

Team members experience aspects of other members' cultures in a fun and supportive way that creates deeper interpersonal understanding and improves the team's overall emotional effectiveness, especially in the areas of communication, decision making, conflict resolution, and motivation. This exercise also demonstrates to the team that their organization values team engagement.

Audience

- Intact teams

Facilitator Competencies

 Moderate

Materials

- Flip-chart paper, easel, and markers

Time Matrix

Exercise	Estimated Time
Part 1: Plan for the cultural fest	30 minutes
Part 2: Hold the cultural fest	60 minutes (depending on team needs and size)
Part 3: Debrief later and reflect on how this supports the team and what potential additional exercises can support the team's positive mood	30 minutes
Total Time	2 hours (depending on team size)

Instructions

This exercise takes place over three meetings. The first is a planning session, the second is the execution of the plan—the fun of the cultural fest—and the third is a chance to debrief and reflect.

Part 1

1. Plan the cultural fest. Begin the first session by discussing the benefits of operating with a positive mood among team members. Discuss the three parts to this exercise and tell them a key part will be the second, which is to have a cultural diversity fest in which all are involved. The fest will be during work hours, as supporting team engagement is a value of the organization.

2. Ask the team to begin planning the event. If you are working with a small team, keep them together to plan. If it's a large team, ask them to break into small groups for fifteen minutes and brainstorm possible components. The items to address include when, where, and what the cultural fest will include. However, while their focus is supported by logistics, the key outcome is to learn more about each other and to have fun. At the cultural fest, each team member will present something about his or her culture. Culture can be defined broadly, and defining what is meant by the term could be part of what the team determines as a part of the planning.

Developing Emotional and Social Intelligence

Each person's presentation should include an action and a story about how the action fits in his or her culture. There are many ways people could present their cultural stories. For example, it could be bringing in a food dish that is passed around to everyone to taste while the presenter tells a story about how earlier family members made the dish in the old country. It could be a folk dance with a story that the dance is a part of someone's culture and that his or her parents met doing the dance. Or it could be a musical instrument that has been an important part of the celebration at family events.

3. Bring everyone back together. Consider the ideas and facilitate agreement on the plan. Include when the event will be held, how much time each person will be given for his or her presentation, and ideas about what is sought in the story. It must include information on how it felt to members of the family to engage in the activity and how it feels now to the presenter to discuss this part of his or her family history.

Part 2

4. Hold the cultural fest. Have fun and be sure each person does talk about family feelings and his or her personal feelings that day. This is a key job for you as facilitator. If a presenter doesn't address these components, ask him or her to do so. For example, "Jose, it's interesting to see the dance! Now tell us how it feels when you do the dance and how it feels when you think of your grandparents doing the dance in Bolivia."

Part 3

5. Facilitate a team discussion within a week after the event to explore what they learned. Also discuss how they felt at the time of the cultural fest and how they feel now as they discuss the topic. Ask them to notice how taking this time during work hours has supported the positive mood of the team. Brainstorm about future actions that can support positive mood.

Tip

Keep what is discussed positive and not too personal so that everyone is comfortable sharing.

EXERCISE 14.2. RECOGNITION CUBES

Purpose

To practice prompt affirmation of positive contributions of team members and to build this practice into a habit.

Thumbnail

20 minutes

Team members use simple materials to regularly record positive team behaviors. Observations are written on pieces of colored paper, attached with a straight pin to a small Styrofoam™ cube or other soft object, and placed in a vessel that is located in a public team area. The vessel is brought to team meetings on a regular basis and the positive acknowledgments attached to each cube are read aloud. The team evaluates this process monthly to explore the impact it is having on their overall team functioning.

Outcomes

As team members practice acknowledging specific, positive behaviors on a regular basis, they experience enhanced appreciation for each other and are more motivated to continue the behaviors. The practice becomes a habit, leading to even greater team functioning.

Audience

- Intact teams

Facilitator Competencies

 Easy

Materials

- Flip-chart paper, easel, and markers
- Items one or more team members will need to find later for the team: one- or two-inch Styrofoam cubes or other small, soft objects; colored heavy stock paper; straight pins; and a vessel large enough to hold all the cubes.

Time Matrix

Exercise	Estimated Time
Discuss acknowledging valuable acts	5 minutes
Explain the process	5 minutes
Practice acknowledging	10 minutes
Total Time	**20 minutes**

Instructions

1. Discuss the connection between taking time to recognize the specific daily events team members do well and an ongoing atmosphere of positive mood for the team.

2. Guide the team to create a strategy for catching teammates in the act of success. Ask for a few volunteers to find a number of small soft objects such as one- or two-inch Styrofoam cubes; small straight pins; pieces of bright colored paper; and a vessel that will hold all the cubes. All of these will go in a common space where the team gathers, such as a break room.

3. Go around the room and ask each team member to name specific positive acts he or she has seen from others on the team. Have each of them name the person who did something well and look at the person when giving the acknowledgement. Then discuss the strategy, which is to give specific and timely recognition to one another when someone does something positive. For example, it might be a kindness, an extra effort on a project, coming in early or staying late, or covering for someone when help is needed.

4. Explain that each person is to stay alert for positive actions from team members. When they see any, ask them to take a minute to write the action and the person's name on a colored piece of paper, stick the paper on a cube with a straight pin, and put it in the vessel. The vessel is then taken to team meetings, cubes will be pulled out, and the acknowledgements read to the full team. This creates a highly positive start to team meetings with a very can-do message, given that what

has been done well will be acknowledged. Recognizing specific and recent actions moves the team away from theory or platitudes and into acknowledging concrete positive actions that frequently occur.

Tip

Ask the team to discuss the process monthly to notice how this direct engagement with positive affirmation is building positive mood and to notice what other benefits they are gaining from it.

EXERCISE 14.3. ROUNDS OF APPRECIATION

Purpose

To help team members create a positive climate by sharing appreciation for what each member brings to the team.

Thumbnail

40 to 60 minutes, depending on team size

Each member answers the following questions about the other members of the team: What do I most appreciate about each team member? Why? They form an inner and an outer circle, pairing up first with those in the other circle, and then with those in the same circle, to share their appreciations one-to-one.

Outcomes

Team members are not always explicit about how each person on the team contributes to the overall value of the team. By sharing what is most appreciated and how that affects the overall team, members gain a deeper awareness of their impact on the team, the positive mood of the team increases, and these strengths can be better leveraged in future interactions.

Audience

- Intact teams
- Individual team members desiring to build skills to take back to the team
- Team leaders

Facilitator Competencies

 Easy

Materials

- Flip-chart paper, easel, and markers
- Pens
- Paper

Time Matrix

Exercise	Estimated Time
Discussion about team climate	5 minutes
Write attributes	5 minutes
Team forms two circles	5 minutes
Rotating pairs share written observations	10 minutes
Discuss the impact in the future	5 minutes
Total Time	**30 minutes**

Instructions

1. Discuss with team members that, in order to bring forward the best that team members have to offer, it is critical that members feel open and emotionally safe with each other. This is accomplished in part by recognizing and validating the characteristics and contributions each member brings, which creates energy and a positive mood on the team. Instead of getting caught in a negative cycle of discussing what is going wrong on a team, a positive cycle can be created by sharing beneficial impacts with each other. Encourage the team to generate ideas about the type of team climate that creates the most positive and energetic mood. Capture those elements on a flip chart.

2. Distribute a list with each team member's name on it to each person to write a characteristic or attribute that he or she most appreciates about each member of the team and why this attribute is valued.

3. Ask the team to form an inner circle and an outer circle. People in the inner circle need to face outward so that they are paired face-to-face with a person in the outer circle.

4. Tell each pair to take turns sharing what they have written about the other team member using the starting phrase, "What I most appreciate about you is _____, and this is why:_____." Share an example to help the person understand their impact. For example, "What I most appreciate about you is your ability to listen. You

Developing Emotional and Social Intelligence

demonstrate that you hear what I have to say, whether you agree with it or not. This makes me feel like a respected member of the team."

5. Inform team members who are receiving the positive feedback that they can ask for some clarification if they are confused, or they can just respond with a simple "Thank you." Instruct the team that, as they learn to better verbalize positive feelings, it is important to acknowledge and show appreciation for a compliment. Guide them to continue to show recognition for each other to build on the sense of can-do attitude that comes from sharing positive feelings.

6. After the first pairs have shared, rotate pairs by having the outer circle move one person clockwise. The newly formed inner/outer circle pairs now share their acknowledgments. Continue this process until the outer circle has rotated a full round.

7. Once everyone in the inner circle has been paired with everyone in the outer circle, have those in the inner circle pair up with each other, and those in the outer circle pair up with each other in order to deliver and receive their observations.

8. After all team members have finished telling each other what they most appreciate and why, discuss the impact of this exercise with the entire team. Also explore with team members ways they might keep this type of positive mood and energy alive in the future.

Tip

As team members develop their ability to be open and honest with each other, they are more likely to use this ability to practice frequent positive remarks toward each other. Increasing a sense of appreciation creates momentum toward purposeful outcomes and builds optimism regarding future challenges.

Conclusion

Opportunities abound to assist your clients in making a sustainable positive difference in their lives by using these thirty-six exercises. We encourage you to think creatively to use this resource in ways that support your effectiveness and to directly help your clients. Thank you for your commitment to developing emotional and social intelligence in the individuals and teams with whom you work. We would be happy to receive feedback on how the exercises work for you. Feel free to comment by email or through our blogs at these addresses:

Marcia Hughes—contact@cgrowth.com; www.cgrowth
.com; www.EITeams.com
Amy Miller—amymiller.executivecoach@gmail.com

Appendix: Feelings Vocabulary

Abandoned
Abashed
Abhor/ing
Able
Abused
Accepted
Accepting
Aching
Adequate
Admired
Adoration
Adored
Adrift
Affection for
Affectionate
Afraid
Aggravated
Aggressive
Aghast
Agitated
Aglow
Agonized
Alarmed
Alert
Alienated

Alive
All alone
Aloof
Amazed
Ambitious
Ambivalent
Amiable
Amorous
Amused
Angry
Anguished
Annoyed
Antagonistic
Anticipating
Anxious
Apart from other
Apathetic
Apologetic
Appalled
Appealing
Appreciated
Appreciative
Apprehensive
Approval
Approved

Ardor
Arrogant
Ashamed
Assured
Astonished
Astounded
At ease
At fault
At loose ends
At peace
At the mercy of
Attached to
Attacked
Attractive
Aversion
Aware
Awed
Awestruck
Awful
Awkward
Bad
Baffled
Balmy
Barren
Bashful

Befuddled
Belittled
Belligerent
Below par
Bemused
Benevolent
Betrayed
Bewildered
Bitter
Blah
Blamed
Bleak
Blew it
Blissful
Blocked
Blue
Boastful
Boiled
Boiling
Bold
Bored
Bothered
Bottled-up
Bound
Brave
Breathless
Brilliant
Brisk
Bugged
Buoyant
Burdened
Burned
Burned up
Bursting
Busy
Butterflies

Calculating
Calm
Capable
Captivated by
Care
Care for
Carefree
Careful
Caring
Cast off
Caught
Caught in a bind
Cautious
Censured
Certain
Chagrined
Charmed
Cheated
Cheerful
Cheery
Cherish
Cherished
Chipper
Choked up
Clever
Close
Cold
Comfortable
Comforted
Compassionate
Compelled
Competent
Competitive
Complacent
Composed
Concentrating

Concern for
Concerned
Concise
Condemned
Confident
Conflict
Conflicted
Confounded
Confused
Congenial
Connected
Conniving
Considered
Consoled
Contemptful
Contemptuous
Contented
Cornered
Courageous
Cowardly
Cranky
Crazy
Creative
Crippled
Criticized
Cross
Crummy
Crushed
Curious
Cut off
Cynical
Daring
Deadened
Dedicated
Defamed
Defeated

Defensive
Deficient
Degraded
Dejected
Delicate
Delighted
Demeaned
Demoralized
Demure
Dependable
Dependent
Depreciated
Depressed
Deserted
Desire/Desirable
Desolate
Despair/ing
Desperate
Despised
Despondent
Destroyed
Determined
Detested
Devastated
Devoted
Different
Disappointed
Disapproving
Disbelief
Discarded
Disconcerted
Disconsolate
Discontented
Discounted
Discouraged
Discredited

Disdainful
Disgraced
Disgusted
Disinterested
Disjointed
Dislike
Dismal
Dismayed
Disorganized
Disparaged
Disparate
Dispassionate
Displeased
Dissatisfied
Dissonant
Distant
Distasteful
Distraught
Distressed
Distrustful
Disturbed
Dominated
Domineering
Done for
Doomed
Doubtful
Down
Downcast
Drained
Dreadful
Dreamy
Dreary
Dubious
Dull
Dumbfounded
Dynamic

Eager
Easy
Easygoing
Eavesdropping
Ecstatic
Edgy
Effective
Efficient
Egotistical
Elated
Elation
Elevated
Emasculated
Embarrassed
Emboldened
Empathetic
Empty
Enamored
Enchanted
Encouraged
Energetic
Enervated
Enmity
Enraged
Enthralled
Enthusiastic
Envious
Erased
Esteemed
Estranged
Estrangement
Euphoric
Evasive
Exalted
Exasperated
Excited

Excluded
Exercised
Exhausted
Exhilarated
Expectant
Exposed
Extravagant
Extroverted
Fantastic
Fascinated
Fatigues
Fear
Fearful
Fearless
Fed-up
Feeble
Festive
Fidgety
Fiendish
Fiery
Finished
Firm
Flat
Flustered
Foggy
Fond
Foolhardy
Foolish
Forceful
Forgetful
Forgiving
Forlorn
Forsaken
Frantic
Free
Friendly

Frightened
Frisky
Frustrated
Fulfilled
Full
Full of questions
Fuming
Furious
Futile
Galled
Gay
Generous
Gentle
Giddy
Giving
Glad
Gleeful
Gloomy
Glowing
Glum
Going around in
     circles
Good
Good for nothing
Gossipy
Graceful
Gratified
Great
Greedy
Grief
Grief-stricken
Grieved
Grieving
Grim
Grouchy
Grumpy

Guilty
Gutless
Hacked
Happiness
Happy
Harassed
Hard
Hardy
Hate
Hateful
Hatred
Heavy-hearted
Helpful
Helpless
Heroic
Hesitant
High
Hilarious
Hold dear
Hollow
Homesick
Hopeful
Hopeless
Horny
Horrible
Horrified
Hostile
Hot
Humble
Humiliated
Humorous
Hung over
Hurt
Hysterical
Identification
Idiotic

Idolize
Ignored
Ill at ease
Immobilized
Impatient
Important
Imposed upon
Impotent
Impressed
Impulsive
In a bind
In a dilemma
Inn a quandary
In despair
In error
In high spirits
In the dumps
Inadequate
Incapable
Incompetent
Incomplete
Indecisive
Independent
Indifferent
Indignant
Ineffective
Ineffectual
Inept
Infatuated
Inferior
Inflamed
Infuriated
Inhibited
Innocent
Insecure
Insignificant

Insincere
Inspired
Insufficient
Insulated from
  others
Intelligent
Interested
Intimidated
Intrigued
Introverted
Intruded upon
Irate
Irked
Irresistible
Irritated
Isolated
Jazzed
Jealous
Jolly
Jovial
Joyful
Joyous
Jubilant
Jumpy
Keen
Kind
Lacking
  confidence
Laughed at
Lazy
Leery
Left out
Let down
Let out
Lethargic
Liberal

Light
Light-hearted
Like
Like a failure
Liked
Listless
Lively
Loaded
Loathed
Loathing
Locked
Logical
Lonely
Lonesome
Longing
Lost
Lost face
Loud
Lovable
Loved
Love-struck
Loving
Low
Loyal
Lucky
Lustful
Mad
Maligned
Martyred
Marvelous
Mature
Mean
Meditative
Melancholy
Mellow
Merry

Mighty
Minimized
Mischievous
Miserable
Misunderstood
Mixed up
Mocked
Modest
Moody
Mortified
Mournful
Moved
Muddled
Naughty
Nauseated
Neat
Needed
Negative
Neglected
Nervous
Noble
Noisy
Nonchalant
Nostalgic
Numb
Objective
Obstinate
Offended
Ok
On cloud nine
On edge
On the spot
On top of the
    world
Open
Optimistic

Original
Out of sorts
Outraged
Overjoyed
Overlooked
Overwhelmed
Overworked
Pain
Pained
Panicky
Paralyzed
Paranoid
Passionate
Passive
Patient
Patronized
Peaceful
Peeved
Perfectionist
Perplexed
Persecuted
Perturbed
Pessimistic
Petrified
Physical
Pissed off
Pity
Playful
Pleasant
Pleased
Pleasure
Popular
Positive toward
Powerful
Powerless
Preoccupied

Pressured
Prize
Proud
Provoked
Prudish
Pulled
Put down
Put out
Put upon
Puzzled
Questioning
Quiet
Rankled
Reassured
Reborn
Receptive
Refined
Regard
Regarded
Regretful
Rejected
Rejecting
Rejuvenated
Relaxed
Released
Relieved
Religious
Reluctant
Remorseful
Remote
Repelled
Repulsed
Resentful
Resigned
Resolved
Respected

Appendix: Feelings Vocabulary

Responsible
Restful
Revengeful
Revolted
Riding high
Rigid
Ripped
Ripped off
Risky
Rotten
Ruined
Sad
Safe
Satisfied
Scared
Scheming
Scornful
Screwed
Secure
Seductive
Seething
Self-conscious
Selfish
Sensational
Sensitive
Sensual
Serene
Set up
Sexy
Shaky
Shamed
Shameful
Sharp
Sheepish
Shocked
Shook

Shot down
Shy
Sick
Sick at heart
Sickened
Silly
Skeptical
Sluggish
Small
Smoldering
Smothered
Smug
Solitary
Somber
Sophisticated
Sorrowful
Sorry
Sparkling
Spellbound
Spirited
Spiteful
Stage fright
Staggered
Startled
Steamed
Stimulated
Stretched
Strong
Stubborn
Stunned
Stupefied
Stupid
Stymied
Successful
Sulky
Sullen

Sure
Surly
Surprised
Suspicious
Sweaty
Sweet
Sympathetic
Taken for granted
Taken with
Talented
Talkative
Taut
Tearful
Tempted
Tender
Tenderness
    toward
Tense
Terrible
Terrific
Terrified
Terror-stricken
Thoughtful
Threatened
Thrilled
Thunderstruck
Thwarted
Ticked
Tight
Timid
Tired
Tolerant
Torn
Torn up
Tortured
Touched

Touchy
Tragic
Tranquil
Transcended
Transcendent
Trapped
Trapped in time
Treasured
Treated unfairly
Triumphant
Troubled
Trust
Trusted
Trusting
Turned off
Turned on
Two-faced
Ugly
Unable
Unaffected
Unappreciated
Unaware
Unbelieving
Uncertain
Unclear
Uncomfortable
Uncooperative
Undecided
Understanding
Understood
Uneasy
Unfair

Unfit
Unfriendly
Unhappy
Unimportant
Unloved
Unorganized
Unpopular
Unpredictable
Unqualified
Unsure
Untroubled
Up
Upset
Uptight
Used
Useless
Vacant
Vague
Vain
Valiant
Valued
Vengeful
Venturous
Vibrant
Vicious
Victimized
Vindictive
Violated
Violent
Vivacious
Vulnerable
Wanted

Warm
Warm toward
Warm-hearted
Washed up
Wavering
Weak
Wearied
Weary
Weepy
Weighted
Whipped
Wide-awake
Wiped out
Wishy-washy
Withdrawn
Witty
Wonder
Wonderful
Worn-out
Worried
Worship
Worthless
Worthwhile
Worthy
Wounded
Wrathful
Wrenched
Wronged
Yearning
Yielding
Zealous

Resources

Authors' Consulting Services

Collaborative Growth
Marcia Hughes, President
James Terrell, Vice President
P.O. Box 17509
Golden, CO 80402
   (303) 271-0021
   contact@cgrowth.com
   www.cgrowth.com
   www.EITeams.com

Amy L. Miller
Executive Coach/Consultant
P.O. Box 12448
Denver, CO 80212
   (303) 433-3146
   amymiller.executivecoach@gmail.com

Assessments

Team Emotional and Social Intelligence Survey® (TESI®)
Collaborative Growth
P.O. Box 17509
Golden, CO 80402
   (303) 271-0021
   www.EITeams.com
   contact@cgrowth.com
Emotional Intelligence Skills Assessment (EISA)
Leadership Practices Inventory (LPI)
Pfeiffer
989 Market Street, 5th Floor

San Francisco, CA 94103
www.pfeiffer.com
www.lpionline.com

EQ-i®
EQ-360®
Multi-Health Systems, Inc.
P.O. Box 950
North Tonawanda, NY 14120-0950
(800) 456-3003
customerservice@mhs.com
www.mhs.com

Emergenetics
Emergenetics International, Inc.
2 Inverness Drive East, Suite 189
Centennial, CO 80112
(888)-8BRAINS
(888) 827-2467
www.emergenetics.com

Myers-Briggs Type Indicator (MBTI®)
Fundamental Interpersonal Relations Orientation-Behavior (FIRO-B)
CPP, Inc.
1055 Joaquin Road, 2nd Floor
Mountain View, CA 94043
(800) 624-1765
www.cpp.com

Emotional and Social Competency Inventory (ESCI)
EI Hay Group
(800) 729-8074
www.haygroup.com

MSCEIT®
Multi-Health Systems, Inc.
P.O. Box 950
North Tonawanda, NY 14120-0950
(800) 456-3003
customerservice@mhs.com
www.mhs.com

Research and Tools

The following are some of the many sites that provide research and tools for developing EI.

Collaborative Growth

Authors and certifiers for TESI; providers of EQ-i and EQ-360 certification; teambuilding, consulting, and coaching

P.O. Box 17509

Golden, CO 80402

www.cgrowth.com

www.EITeams.com

EI Consortium

The Consortium for Research on Emotional Intelligence in Organizations aids the advancement of research and practice related to emotional intelligence in organizations.

www.eiconsortium.org

FeedbackToGo.com

Online tool for rater feedback and developing effective behaviors

Catalyst Consulting Inc.

Claudia Busch Lee, Ph.D.

20 Keithley Road

Manitou Springs, CO 80829

www.feedbacktogo.com

www.catalystconsulting1.com

Multi Health Systems

Distributes EQ-i, MSCEIT, and supporting products

3770 Victoria Parke Avenue

Toronto, Ontario M2H 3M6

Canada

Pfeiffer

Publisher of materials for trainers and consultants, including the EISA and other EI-related publications

989 Market Street, 5th Floor

San Francisco, CA 94103

www.pfeiffer.com

References

Bar-On, R. (2001). EI and self-actualization. In J. Ciarrochi, J. Forgas, & J. Mayer (Eds.), *Emotional intelligence in everyday life* (p. 92). New York: Psychology Press.

Bar-On, R. (2004). *Bar-On emotional quotient inventory (EQ-i): Technical manual.* Toronto, Ontario: Multi-Health Systems, Inc.

Browning, G. (2006). *Emergenetics: Tap into the new science of success.* New York: HarperCollins.

Frankl, V. (1959, 1992). *Man's search for meaning.* Boston: Beacon Press.

Hughes, M. (2006). *Life's 2% solution: Simple steps to achieve happiness and balance.* Boston: Nicholas Brealey.

Hughes, M., Patterson, L.B., & Terrell, J. (2005). *Emotional intelligence in action.* San Francisco: Pfeiffer.

Hughes, M., & Terrell, J. (2007). *The emotionally intelligent team.* San Francisco: Jossey-Bass.

Hughes, M., & Terrell, J. B. (2009). *Team emotional and social intelligence: Facilitator's guide. TESI short.* San Francisco: Pfeiffer.

Hughes, M., Thompson, H.L., & Terrell, J.B. (Eds.). (2009). *The handbook for developing emotional and social intelligence: Best practices, case studies and strategies.* San Francisco: Pfeiffer.

Kouzes, J.M., & Posner, B.Z. (2007). *Leadership challenge* (4th ed.). San Francisco: Jossey-Bass.

Myers, I.B. (1998). *Introduction to type* (6th ed.). Palo Alto, CA: CPP, Inc.

Stein, S., Mann, D., Papadogiannis, P., & Gordon, W. (2009). *Emotional intelligence skills assessment: Facilitator's guide.* San Francisco: Pfeiffer.

Terrell, J., & Hughes, M. (2008). *A coach's guide to emotional and social intelligence.* San Francisco: Pfeiffer.

Waterman, J., & Rogers, J. (2004). *Introduction to the FIRO-B instrument.* Palo Alto, CA: CPP, Inc.

About the Authors

Marcia Hughes, J.D., M.A., is president of Collaborative Growth®, L.L.C., and serves as a strategic communications partner for teams and their leaders in organizations that value high performers. She weaves her expertise in emotional intelligence throughout her consulting work, facilitation, team building, and workshops to help people motivate themselves and communicate more effectively with others. Her keynotes are built around powerful stories of how success can grow when people work collaboratively. Marcia and her partner, James Terrell, are authors of *The Team Emotional and Social Intelligence Survey®* (TESI®), an online team assessment, and the TESI Short, published by Pfeiffer. She is co-editor of *The Handbook for Developing Emotional Intelligence* (2009), co-author of *A Facilitator's Guide to Team Emotional and Social Intelligence, (2009), A Coach's Guide for Emotional Intelligence* (2008), *The Emotionally Intelligent Team* (2007), *Emotional Intelligence in Action (2005)*, and author of *Life's 2% Solution* (2006). Marcia works with many diverse clients, including American Express, Medtronic, the World Bank, the Central Intelligence Agency, and the Department of Agriculture.

Marcia is a member of the Consortium for Research on Emotional Intelligence in Organizations (CREIO) and is a certified trainer in the TESI, and the EQ-i® and EQ-360®. She provides train-the-trainer training and coaching in powerful EI delivery. Her efforts to improve productivity in the workplace through strategic communication grew out of a distinguished career in law, where her firm specialized in complex public policy matters. She also served as an assistant attorney general and clerked on the 10th Circuit Court of Appeals for the Honorable William E. Doyle.

Amy Miller, M.A., is an executive coach and leadership consultant in private practice in Denver, Colorado. She has coached hundreds of executives and mid-level managers in corporate, governmental, and non-profit organizations to help them set and achieve meaningful, ambitious goals for themselves and their organizations. She previously has held leadership positions in a variety of industries and has led organizations through times of great financial and structural change, including start-ups and transitional periods of growth as well as downsizing. She has hired and supervised hundreds of employees, mediated many high-conflict workplace situations, and administered marketing, personnel, and human resource functions. She has served as policy advisor to executives and boards of directors and has extensive experience in coaching global corporate and governmental leaders in developing conflict management skills. She is skilled in utilizing a variety of assessments, including 360-degree, emotional intelligence, work style, creativity, change dynamics, personality, and conflict management instruments, to inform her clients' individual and organizational growth. She has deep respect for the challenges leaders face and has a lifelong commitment to helping leaders and organizations create conditions that best and fully integrate the intellectual and emotional talents individuals bring to their work. Her efforts to foster effective leadership have also included volunteer work as a board member for an educational/community non-profit organization as well as serving on future scholar selection committees for university leadership programs.